LESSONS IN LOSS
AND LIVING

LESSONS IN LOSS AND LIVING

Hope and Guidance for Confronting Serious Illness and Grief

Michele A. Reiss, Ph.D.

HYPERION
·····
NEW YORK

Library of Congress Cataloging-in-Publication Data

Reiss, Michele.
   Lessons in loss and living : hope and guidance for confronting serious illness and
grief / Michele Reiss.
      p. cm.
   ISBN 978-1-4013-2366-0
   1. Death—Psychological aspects.   2. Sick—Psychological aspects.   3. Grief.
4. Loss (Psychology)   I. Title.
   BF789.D4R448 2011
   155.9'37—dc22

                                                                    2010031846

Hyperion books are available for special promotions and premiums.
For details contact the HarperCollins Special Markets Department
in the New York office at 212-207-7528, fax 212-207-7222,
or email spsales@harpercollins.com.

Book design by Jo Anne Metsch

FIRST EDITION

10 9 8 7 6 5 4 3 2 1

| SUSTAINABLE FORESTRY INITIATIVE | Certified Fiber Sourcing www.sfiprogram.org |

THIS LABEL APPLIES TO TEXT STOCK

We try to produce the most beautiful books possible, and we are also extremely concerned about the impact of our manufacturing process on the forests of the world and
the environment as a whole. Accordingly, we've made sure that all of the paper
we use has been certified as coming from forests that are managed to ensure the protec-
tion of the people and wildlife dependent upon them.

Each of the stories in this book is about an amazing person I know or have known. In most instances their identifying characteristics have been altered for privacy reasons, but I believe their grace and spirit shine through. Whether colleague, friend, family member, or client, I have been blessed to have each of these people in my life. And this book is dedicated to all of them.

CONTENTS

FOREWORD

In the late summer of 2006, my husband and Carnegie Mellon professor Dr. Randy Pausch was diagnosed with pancreatic cancer. At the time, Randy and I were living a dream life together. We had two young sons and a new baby girl. We were putting an addition onto the house where we planned to raise our children. We loved each other and the world that we had created for ourselves.

When Randy was told that he might have only three to six months to live, our dream life came to a crashing halt. I tried to adjust to the new reality: I would have to raise our children alone, in the house where Randy and I were supposed to grow old together. Meanwhile, Randy coped with the ordeal of cancer symptoms, cancer treatments, and the very real fear of possibly imminent death. Put all of this together, and you have a recipe for disaster.

Randy and I realized the negative impact that all of this stress was having on our lives, our love, and our family. We tried working through these problems together, but without success. Randy had consulted with some of the best and brightest specialists to help improve his odds of beating one of the most fatal cancers. He had an impressive health-care team comprised of oncologists, surgeons, radiologists, and nurses, who joined us in our battle against cancer. However, we had overlooked the psychological aspect of the disease. Cancer doesn't just do physical damage. It erodes your ability to love and enjoy life. It can make you miss out on the precious living time that you have left and make you act and feel like you're dead, when you're still very much alive. You can probably replace the word "cancer" with almost any other terrible challenge that life can dish up to you. But our experience was with pancreatic cancer.

Luckily, our oncologist recommended a local psychotherapist who works mainly with folks whose lives are affected by cancer or other life-threatening illnesses. In the past, Randy hadn't been a great believer in the benefits of counseling, regardless of the situation. He perceived that you could and should solve your own problems. However, he and I realized that we were in a situation where the problems were far greater than our abilities, and the stakes were too high to ignore any possible avenues that might benefit our young children and ourselves.

So it was with trepidation that we started working with Dr. Michele Reiss. Ultimately, we became her biggest fans. Dr. Reiss helped us to continue to live and not shut down. She helped us to set our life priorities and make the best choices we could, based on the information that we had at any given moment in time. We were able to express our hurt to each other and continue to love and support each other throughout each cancer ordeal. We were able to support our children and create a safe and loving environment for them, even when we were emotionally and physically spent by the stresses of living with cancer. All of these positives came from working with Dr. Reiss as we confronted each new challenge.

Unfortunately, not every cancer program has a psychotherapist as part of their team. Lots of folks who could truly benefit from counseling during times of extreme duress often go without. Dr. Reiss has written down the kind of guidance that Randy and I found so helpful during our ordeal. I believe that her work will empower you, the reader, to better approach the challenges facing you in life, whether it be cancer or grief, or something else, and to make choices that will ultimately lead to a happier life.

Bad things are going to happen to you in life. It's a simple fact. But people who learn to pick up the pieces of their broken dreams and make something else out of them, maybe even a beautiful stained-glass window, will become the heroes in their own life stories.

—JAI PAUSCH

PREFACE

I am a psychotherapist who works with individuals and families coping with life-threatening medical illnesses. Recently, I gained public acknowledgment as the therapist who worked with Dr. Randy Pausch and his wife, Jai. However, I have been doing this work along with other types of therapy and teaching for more than thirty years. I have been blessed to have the opportunity to do work that I love and find intensely gratifying.

Many years ago, I was doing therapy with a very bright but defensive six-year-old boy. Tommy had been recently diagnosed with leukemia and was about to start chemotherapy. Tommy was tall for his age, thin, and pale. His eyes were bright with fear. I was trying, somewhat unsuccessfully, to engage him in a conversation in order to get a better sense of his fears and concerns. I finally gave up on the direct approach and instead asked him to imagine that I had a magic wand and had the ability to grant him three wishes. Tommy looked thoughtful for a minute, and then smiled and replied, "I only need one wish. I want my own wand."

Tommy was smarter than his therapist that day. And he was right. I have no magic cures up my sleeves for either terminal illness or acute grief. I work in the realm of caring, not curing. My hope is to help each seriously ill person confront their life-threatening illness in such a way that they are still able to live fully and genuinely for as long as possible. My goals for their families are to help them find the strength that they will need to bear witness to their loved ones' illness; and then, if needed, to help them find a way to not only survive their grief but to also find a place for it so that they can move on to perhaps different but still fulfilling lives. The power for this emotional healing lies within each person who enters my office. I simply try to find the right tools and strategies to maximize each individual's own hidden or not-so-hidden strengths. I want all of my clients to have their own magic wands.

As many readers may already know, Dr. Randy Pausch was a forty-seven-year-old university professor, husband of the lovely Jai Pausch, and father of three very beautiful young children. Dr. Pausch was diagnosed with advanced pancreatic cancer and given a few months to live. Randy outlived that original dire prediction and spent the last year of his life inspiring the rest of us to be brave enough to live out our dreams.

I often give talks to both professional and lay audiences about various topics related to the end of life and bereavement. Routinely, several kind and concerned audience members will stop by afterward to ask how I can possibly do such important but depressing and ultimately futile work. I regularly respond that although my life's work is often sad and usually fairly intense, it is also truly inspiring.

After all, I get to work with heroes like Randy and Jai Pausch. I get to work with individuals who are facing the unimaginable and who find the energy to fight the good fight; to search their psyches and their souls to find the best way to live the rest of their possibly limited life spans with as much grace, courage, and love as possible.

Illness and grief are inevitable life experiences. All of us, regardless of our cultural, spiritual, or socioeconomic standing will sooner or later have to cope with the challenges of a life-threatening illness or loss of a loved one. I'd like to take this opportunity to share some of the lessons that I've learned from the very special people I have had the honor of working with. I've often thought of these lessons as their last gifts to me, but now the teacher in me gets to share these final gifts and lessons with all of you.

> *My candle burns at both ends;*
> *It will not last the night;*
> *But, ah, my foes, and, oh, my friends—*
> *It gives a lovely light!*
>
> —EDNA ST. VINCENT MILLAY

PART ONE

Serious Illness:
Issues and Opportunities

Chapter One

BAD
NEWS

*Life is not about waiting for the storm to pass;
it is about learning to dance in the rain.*

—AUTHOR UNKNOWN

FIRST LESSONS

My first lessons about death and dying happened a very long time ago. I was starting college, studying nursing. Within eighteen months of my first day as a college student, three of my grandparents died of cancer. So I took classes on death and dying, started taking care of cancer patients, and made frequent trips home to visit hospital rooms and attend funerals. It was pretty stressful, but of course I now realize that I had the easy part. My parents were juggling the complex responsibilities of caring for my two younger brothers while visiting three different hospitals and eventually arranging three different funerals; not to mention their need to attend to their own and their spouse's grief.

A number of my first hospital patients and my three ill grandparents had something besides cancer in common. None of them knew about their cancer diagnosis. This was confusing and problematic for me as a young and very idealistic nursing student, because it was counter to what I was learning in my Death and Dying classroom.

In class we were studying the seminal work of Dr. Elisabeth Kübler-Ross, who spent several years interviewing dying patients and eventually wrote the first of several influential books on her research. Her first book, published in 1969, entitled *On Death and Dying,* informed its readers that dying patients often sense that they are dying whether officially informed or not, and that they have a lot to say about their dying experience.

But up until the late '60s and early '70s, it was common medical practice to inform family members about their loved one's terminal prognosis, but not the person doing the dying. This was a well-intentioned, paternalistic attempt to protect the dying person from unnecessary hopelessness and despair. Unfortunately, this protective but deceptive practice also prevented families such as my own and my early patients' from saying good-bye or addressing any unfinished business.

During my early career as a nurse and later as a therapist, I have watched this particular clinical pendulum swing in the opposite direction. Today's emphasis is on patients' rights. Today patients are consumers, and the current trend is toward full disclosure. We are all entitled to be fully informed about our illness and its treatment options, just as we are legally entitled to participate in decisions about the medical interventions to be used or not used at the end of life.

So as a young nursing student I argued passionately, as only the young and inexperienced can argue, about the unmet needs of my grandparents and my first patients. I argued with my clinical instructors, and I argued with my poor parents. Paradoxically, today as I teach my own classes on death and dying, I now urge the young physicians in my audience to realize that although full disclosure is a good thing, it doesn't have to be delivered like a sledgehammer.

BAD NEWS: GIVING AND RECEIVING

Bad news should be dosed as tolerated. Bad news should be delivered privately and kindly. Bad news should be spoken in words that a patient or family member can readily understand. No matter how busy the doctor giving you the bad news is, there should be time for silence, time for tears, and time for questions. After all, we are talking about conversations that usually last minutes, but change lives forever.

I also teach that almost any initial emotional reaction to bad news is an OK one. How each of us receives bad news will depend on many personal variables. Our responses will be influenced by our respective personalities, along with any prior experiences we may have had with similar scenarios and possibly our cultural or spiritual context.

Our individual perception of the meaning of the bad news will also play an important role in how we react both initially and thereafter. For example, I remember a young athlete bursting into tears after being told that her knee operation had been a glowing success. Everyone in the room was bewildered by the tearful reply to such good news. It was a far better operative outcome than had been anticipated. Sally was a competitive skier and had taken a horrible fall. It had been feared she would be permanently disabled. Haltingly, our young patient was able to explain that the upcoming six months of physical therapy and rehab would preclude any chance of her competing in the pre-Olympic trials that she had previously qualified for. From her perspective, the dream of a lifetime had just been crushed.

There are some situations that none of us can be totally prepared for, and you can only do the best you can in the moment. Hearing this kind of bad news is one of those moments. Over the years, I have seen and heard the feared diagnosis of cancer shared many times. Each time is unique, but there is always a moment when it seems as if everyone in the room is holding his or her breath, waiting for the pieces of the conversation to fall together.

Well-trained physicians will often deliver what we call a "warning shot" to give the receivers of the bad news a moment to focus and prepare themselves. It usually goes something like, "I'm very sorry, Mr. Jones, but I'm afraid that I don't have good news for you today." Upon hearing bad news, some people respond with shocked or stoic silence and just thank the doctor for his or her time. Others look visibly shaken and upset. Some people start sobbing. Others start asking a lot of fairly specific questions. So in fairness, doctors giving bad news never quite know what they will have to react to. Most doctors I know are truly touched and saddened by these moments, despite having encountered them fairly often.

Hearing and actually absorbing bad news requires us to process the information both emotionally and cognitively. Some of us can do both at the same time, but many of us do one form of processing and then the other. So if you're one of the rapid-fire question askers, please remember to find time a bit later to let your emotions in, preferably with a good friend or loved one at your side. If the initial response was more emotional or just plain overwhelmed, find time after this first conversation to write down a list of questions that you might want to ask the next time. Family members and friends can help to create a thorough list of meaningful and practical questions.

NOT PART OF THE PLAN

Roger was a fifty-year-old businessman. His hair was salt-and-pepper; his build was short and stocky. His smile was automatic but less than genuine; it was a smile that never reached his eyes. Roger was married and he and his wife had no children. His wife was often in his hospital room, but they never seemed to talk, perhaps because Roger was usually on the phone conducting business.

Roger had smoked cigarettes most of his adult life. He had started coughing, spitting up blood, and having sporadic difficulty breathing several months prior to this hospitalization, but he had been "too busy" to take the time off from work to look into the possible causes of his recent physical distress. Finally, his distraught wife had convinced him to go to the doctor. He was hospitalized immediately and the resulting diagnostic workup had revealed an aggressive lung cancer.

I accompanied Roger's doctor when it was time to tell this busy man and his worried, quiet wife the bad news. Roger predictably kept the doctor waiting several minutes while he finished up the most recent business phone call. He then nodded impatiently as the doctor shared the worrisome test results. Roger's only questions had to do with scheduling issues. His wife was tearful, but once again silent.

Several times later that afternoon, I stuck my head into Roger's room to see if he needed anything. His wife had gone home, but he was still on the phone, seemingly discussing finances of some sort. Just before I was ready to leave the hospital, I once again peeked into Roger's patient-room-turned-office. This last time, the room was darkened and I glimpsed Roger sitting by the window with his head bowed in his hands. I took a seat next to him. He looked up and this time there was no smile, just pain and sadness in his eyes. In the lonely twilight of that difficult day, Roger had finally slowed down enough to meet up with his feelings. We talked for only about ten minutes, although it felt longer.

Roger had spent the afternoon, after his wife left, conversing with his financial advisor to make sure his wife would be cared for should his upcoming chemotherapy treatment fail. In talking with Roger, I learned that his father had been a nice man, but an inept businessman. Roger's father had died without providing for either his wife or only son. Roger had been determined to prove his worth as a family man. He was undoubtedly a successful businessman and had provided an affluent lifestyle for his spouse, although reportedly his wife often told him that she would be far happier with fewer things in order to have more time with him. His plan had been to work extraordinarily hard but retire by his mid-fifties. He would then devote time to his wife and leisure activities. The afternoon's bad news had not been part of the plan.

After ten minutes of quiet conversation, Roger patted my hand and thanked me for listening but clearly indicated that our time was over. As I stood up, I suggested that Roger and his wife might benefit from another, less rushed, meeting with their physician so that they could both better understand what lay ahead and how to help each other prepare for it. To my surprise, he agreed and asked me to leave a message requesting such a meeting with his doctor for the next day. Roger was discharged the following afternoon. His chemotherapy treatments would occur elsewhere. I didn't speak to him again, but I did notice that as he and his wife were getting into the hospital elevator, they were holding hands.

Roger's story reminds me that sometimes bad news needs to be delivered more than once to be truly heard and absorbed.

We all need and deserve time to process life-changing events. Roger's story also reflects how thoroughly complicated the human psyche can be. Roger was both the officious, insensitive businessman and the driven, overcompensating son of a perceived failure of a father. Roger was not a bad man, but he may have been a misguided one. I have often wondered if the sad news of that day truly brought Roger and his wife closer. I hope so.

AN INTENSE CATHARSIS

Kim was a thirty-two-year-old divorced mother of two little girls ages three and five. She was only about five foot two, but she was a presence to be reckoned with. Her curly, long hair was dyed a bright red. Her fingernails and toenails were polished in a similarly eye-catching hue. Her voice was distinctive and easily heard outside of her hospital room.

Kim was a hard worker and a highly stressed single parent. Her divorce had gone badly and she was working long hours as a secretary, barely making financial ends meet as she struggled to provide for herself and her two young daughters. Her parents were both deceased, and one remaining sibling lived far away. Kim could be brusque and demanding. Kim could also be described as a high-strung, moody woman. She was easily upset, and she cried readily and often. Kim had been in the hospital for only five days, but her highly emotional demeanor and seemingly insatiable need for attention and reassurance was wearing out both her attending physician and the floor nurses.

Kim had been experiencing fatigue, weakness, and other nonspecific but disruptive symptoms for more than a year. Each time she started working with her physician to uncover the cause of her distress, either her symptoms would improve or she would become too busy with the chores involved in working and rearing two young children alone. Months would go by, and then Kim would return to her physician and start the process all over again. This time, her doctor had convinced her to come into the hospital for several days in the hopes of avoiding the prior pattern of unintentional noncompliance. Recent scans had discovered the cause of Kim's off-again, on-again symptoms: She had Multiple Sclerosis (MS).

Multiple Sclerosis is a degenerative neurological illness with a variable but inevitably progressive course. For some people, this illness progresses very, very slowly, but for others, its disabling effects are experienced within a relatively short time. Kim's physician had been hoping that her vague symptoms would be stress-related and of no serious medical import. Everyone was concerned about how this highly emotive and stressed-out woman would respond to such difficult news.

Kim's physician tried to deliver his bad news as softly and compassionately as possible. Kim was instantaneously hysterical. She sobbed about her hard and unfair life. She railed about how others less deserving had lives filled with unneeded blessings. She leaped off the worst-case-scenario bridge of negative expectations and was convinced that within months she would be wheelchair-bound and that she and her daughters would probably starve to death, unloved and unnoticed.

Kim's initial reaction was more dramatic than most. It was distressing and exhausting for all involved, including, of course, Kim. And despite everyone's efforts to provide the needed education and support, it continued for two more days. Kim pretty much cried day and night. She told anyone who would listen about her undeserved misfortune and its probable dire consequences. And then she stopped.

On the third day, a tired-looking and more subdued Kim requested a meeting with one of the hospital social workers so that she could start exploring any available resources for herself and her daughters. She asked for some educational pamphlets on her disease, and she asked for some advice on how to talk to her daughters about this unfortunate turn of events when she returned home.

I don't think any singular therapeutic intervention caused Kim to shift from her dramatic to problem-solving stance. Several of us had tried to patiently and empathetically listen to Kim's tirade before gently suggesting that some of her emotional energies needed to be redirected toward how to care for herself and her daughters, despite life's recent unfairness. Perhaps she just needed a fairly intense catharsis before moving forward.

Kim's dramatic reaction was the polar opposite of Roger's initial businesslike reaction. Yet both of these disparate personalities eventually got where they needed to go. Roger opened up emotionally, and hopefully let both his feelings and his wife into his unplanned-for new world. And Kim found the inner strength to move past her fear-driven emotional breakdown and returned to the task of caring for her two children as best she could. Both Kim and Roger, despite their inherent differences, just needed time and someone to listen.

EDUCATED ESTIMATES

Hearing bad news is inevitably distressing, no matter how skillfully it has been delivered or how adeptly it has been processed. However, despite truly amazing advances in medical research and technology, any individual's prognosis is at best a very educated estimate, not a literal script. Many of the patients

I have worked with have outlived their original prognoses, sometimes by months and sometimes much longer. Others have not.

Many years ago, a well-known university sociology professor in my community was diagnosed with an advanced breast cancer and given approximately two years to live. This bright and charming woman chose to keep teaching, and she included many of her own experiences as a cancer patient in her undergraduate lesson plans. Students flocked to enroll in her classes for good reason; she was a good teacher and a great source of inspiration. She lived about nine months beyond her original prognostic estimate. She once shared with a colleague that the last nine months were the hardest because she felt that she was living on borrowed time. This comment depicts the incredible courage it takes to confront the powerful uncertainty of our own mortality and yet decide to work, love, and live another day.

Earlier in my career, I worked with both children and adults who had been diagnosed with cancer. One morning I was walking through a local hospital's pediatric ward and encountered an incredibly distraught couple. They were standing in a busy hallway and looked as if they could easily fall over at any moment. I went over, introduced myself, and asked if I could help in some way. They tearfully shared that the hospital radiologist had just bumped into them in the very same hallway. He had taken a moment to inform them that their eight-year-old daughter's imaging studies had shown a rare brain tumor. This physician had consulted the article he was just reading to inform them that their only child's life expectancy was probably within the five-year range.

I forgot about the meeting that I had been heading to, and the three of us went for coffee. We became fast friends, and I worked with this wonderful couple and their ill daughter, Molly, for the next eight years. Unfortunately, I lost track of this special family when I began working at a different hospital and they relocated out of town. Although Molly had lived long past her original prognosis, she had been fairly ill much of the time that we had worked together. I assumed that at some point in time, the cancer had won, but I had no way of knowing for sure.

A year ago, I was in another hospital hallway and encountered an old colleague from my original place of employment. We chatted about old friends, and she eventually asked me if I had heard from the mother of this particular cancer patient. I replied that sadly we had lost touch years ago. My colleague then shared that she had recently run into my old friend; she had come back into town to attend Molly's wedding.

Uncertainty can be a good thing sometimes.

SAYING GOOD-BYE

The first of my three grandparents to die was my favorite: my father's mother. Like my other grandparents, she had not been told of her cancer diagnosis. Although I disagreed, I respected my father's wishes and went along with the ruse. It was the winter holiday break of my freshman year at college. My grandmother was quite ill, but she was at home. I was sitting quietly in her bedroom as she slept. We were alone, which was unusual.

It was just about time for me to leave and begin the trek back to school when my grandmother stirred and opened her eyes. She smiled weakly and asked when I would be returning home again. I replied that my next break wasn't until spring.

She sighed sadly and quietly whispered, "I'm not sure I can make it that long." I took a deep breath and whispered back, "I know, and I'll miss you. I love you very much." She took my hand, looked at me with her piercing blue eyes, and said, "Thank you." I never saw her again. She died two days before my spring break, but I will be forever grateful for her last gift to me: the gift of saying good-bye.

The opportunity to say good-bye to a loved one is as precious as it is heartbreaking.

As I start to write this book, my father is now eighty-nine years old and suffering from advanced Parkinson's disease. His mind is still intact, but his body continues to fail him. We talk on the phone nightly. We talk as father and daughter; we talk as friends. He talks openly, honestly, and bravely about this sad, frustrating twilight time of his life. We talk about his feelings about dying and how much he misses my mom. We have come full circle. I'm grateful for that gift too.

Chapter Two

UNFINISHED BUSINESS

Not every illness can be cured. We can however,
make use of an illness to help us redirect our lives.

—BERNIE S. SIEGEL, M.D.,
Peace, Love and Healing

A MAN OF FEW WORDS

Years after my grandmother died, I was a young therapist providing psychological services for the oncology department of a nearby hospital. Each new patient was a challenge and a lesson to be learned. All of these patients were seriously ill, but most were eager and grateful for any guidance or support that I could offer. There was, however, a memorable exception to this general rule.

Mr. Schmidt was sixty-four years old, but looked much older. He had lived a hard life. Reportedly he had been an alcoholic who was estranged from his ex-wife and their daughter. He had no visitors during his several-week stay at the hospital. Mr. Schmidt was not only socially isolated, he was unlucky. He had been diagnosed with a rare but very aggressive cancer. His prognosis was considered dismal at best. Mr. Schmidt had agreed to a brief trial of aggressive chemotherapy in hopes of slowing the rapid spread of his tumor. The relative odds of the chemotherapy extending his life in any meaningful way were considered quite small. Discussion among the staff had already started about how to best provide support to Mr. Schmidt upon discharge, because it was assumed that he would be dying alone.

John Schmidt was a man of few words. He avoided eye contact; he shrugged his shoulders and tended to respond to my questions with monosyllabic yeses or nos. One of his rare complete sentences came after I introduced myself, at which point he brusquely commented, "I don't see what talking about stuff is going to do; it can't change anything." Secretly I sort of agreed with him, but we were both wrong that first day.

I visited Mr. Schmidt in his lonely corner room every day for the next three weeks. I didn't look forward to those daily sessions. I felt useless and stymied. I talked; he didn't seem to listen. I asked questions that he either didn't answer or answered incompletely at best.

By the end of the first week, I had confirmed that Mr. Schmidt was truly alone. He had been a "mean drunk"; his wife had divorced him and moved away with their young daughter. His daughter had eventually moved to the West Coast. Mr. Schmidt thought she might be married with a child of her own, but he wasn't sure. Mr. Schmidt had not had any contact with either his ex-wife or daughter for more than twenty years. When asked about trying to contact them due to his life-threatening illness, he adamantly responded, "They're better off without me. Leave it alone."

By the second week, Mr. Schmidt was weakened by his daily chemotherapy and even less interested in talking. So I did the talking and he just lay there. I had resigned myself to the fact that Mr. Schmidt just wasn't a good therapy candidate, but the least I could do was keep him company and treat him with kindness, despite his best efforts to offend me.

Luckily for me, right outside that corner room's window an old house was slowly being torn down to make room for an expanded parking lot. The hospital was rife with rumors about the family who had once lived in that old house and how much money they may have been offered to allow the hospital to expand its overcrowded boundaries. Also luckily for me, Mr. Schmidt had worked in construction. So I talked about the family who used to live in the old house, and he perked up and started to tell me about how the house had originally been constructed and what was involved in tearing it down. I briefly wondered if this ongoing, almost animated conversation about the old house was a clinical metaphor for Mr. Schmidt's dying process, but then I dismissed the thought as overly imaginative.

By the end of the third week, it was apparent that chemotherapy had failed to yield any positive result. The old house was now mostly rubble, and reportedly its family had relocated to a newer domicile. Mr. Schmidt was discharged with home-care support until the time he would no longer be able to live independently, at which point hospice would be involved. I stopped by to wish him well, but his bed was empty; he had already left. I felt sad, but also relieved that I wouldn't have to sit through those frustrating daily sessions anymore.

Six weeks later, I was lunching with colleagues at a local cafeteria across the street from the hospital. As I was paying my check, someone tapped me on the shoulder. It was a man I didn't recognize until he spoke. It was Mr. Schmidt, with his distinctive, gruff voice. He looked different in street clothes instead of hospital garb. He glanced at me briefly, then cast his eyes downward and muttered, "Just wanted to say thank you."

I was more than a little surprised, but mostly I was confused.

"Thank me for what, Mr. Schmidt?" He replied in a somewhat exasperated tone, "I have a grandson. You know how you pestered me to contact my daughter? Well, I did. She and her husband are staying with me until . . . You know, until it's over. I guess she forgave me. I don't know why, but she did. My daughter's a good parent, not like me. It's nice. So thanks." After verbalizing more words than I had heard him speak in our three weeks together, Mr. Schmidt simply turned and walked away. Two months later, I heard that he had died at home in the presence of his daughter and a hospice worker.

Mr. Schmidt's decision to seek reconciliation with his daughter surprised me greatly for several reasons. First of all, my initial recommendation was greeted with a very strong negative response. Any other time that I raised the possibility of contacting either old friends or estranged family members, Mr. Schmidt simply ignored me. (I do think that "pestering" is too strong a word for my tendency to make what I viewed as a sound therapeutic suggestion, more than once. But perhaps the line between needed repetition and nagging is in the eye of the beholder.) Secondly, during his entire hospital stay, Mr. Schmidt consistently rebuffed any and all interpersonal overtures. He was clearly not a "people person."

ARE YOU LISTENING?

Years later, experiences as both a therapist and a parent have taught me that sometimes people are listening to what you say, even when they don't seem to be. This is true particularly when the person on the receiving end of the conversation is both defensive and vulnerable at the same time.

Teenagers are a prime example. In our society, adolescence

is a prolonged and confusing developmental progression from childhood to young adulthood. Teens are in the unenviable position of being part child and part adult at the same time. Their moods and behaviors can reflect this developmental inconsistency in annoying and concerning ways. Many adolescents take risks that they shouldn't take, just to prove that they are old enough to do so. At the same time, these same teens may cling desperately to similarly confused peers in order to mask their true lack of readiness for real independence.

My beautiful grown therapist daughter, Jen, was my best teacher about this dance of being heard despite all indications to the contrary. One particular afternoon, I tried to confront her after a series of near-miss adolescent adventures. I was worried sick about her; she was furious with me because I dared to challenge her fragile bid for independence. I talked, and, like Mr. Schmidt, she looked away and seemed not to hear a word that I said. I told her how much I loved her but also how worried I was. I told her that I would fight to guide and protect her, even if she hated me for it, because I loved her too much not to. I told her that I would keep loving and trying to protect her no matter how hard she pushed me away, and that I would continue to do so until I was sure she loved herself enough to keep safe. I poured my maternal heart out during that conversation. When I was through, she shrugged, muttered "Whatever," and walked away. I still remember how exhausted, defeated, and heartbroken I felt after that failed conversation.

My daughter survived her adolescence, despite my seemingly ineffective parental intervention. She stumbled, but always picked herself up. Eventually, she found her way toward becoming the lovely woman and skilled therapist that she is today.

Not too long ago, we were spending a mother-daughter day

lunching, shopping, and reminiscing. We were busy talking and laughing when all of a sudden she looked directly at me and asked, "Do you remember that fight we had in the kitchen that afternoon?" I knew exactly what she was talking about. I nodded, remembering all too vividly that sad, scary moment. Jen smiled gently. "I know that I didn't let you know back then, but that was the day that I knew I'd be OK, because I knew that you wouldn't give up on me no matter what."

Both Mr. Schmidt and my daughter were listening, even though they gave no visible signs of doing so. They simply needed some time and space to come to their own conclusions, without losing face. So when offering well-intended support or suggestions to a vulnerable friend or loved one (for example, someone who is seriously ill or newly bereaved), be patient. Offer your input gently, respectfully, and caringly, but then give the person the time and space to sort things out for themselves. Sometimes, if we speak with compassion and respect, people will hear us even when they don't seem to be listening.

Giving support or advice, whether as a therapist, parent, or loved one, is like planting seeds. You may not know right away whether the seeds will take. But if you're patient and trust the process, perhaps something beautiful will grow.

PERSONAL MEANING

Mr. Schmidt's decision to reach out to the daughter he had abandoned was inconsistent with how he had lived much of his life. Yet during the last months of his life, this troubled man found the strength and courage to confront his past. He risked rejection instead of avoiding or initiating it. Why? Perhaps he was simply afraid of the all-too-real prospect of dying alone.

Or perhaps the solitude of his dying made him confront for the first time the unnecessary loneliness of his life.

The search for personal meaning is one way that many of us attempt to cope with tragedy or crisis. We ask why. We try to make sense out of something that we either had not anticipated or feel unprepared for. Some people turn to religion or faith during this search for meaning, and others seek elsewhere. We want to believe that there is some good reason for whatever is happening or will happen to us, because the possibility that there is no reason is too hard to bear.

Never is the need for personal meaning stronger than when someone is confronting his or her own mortality. Those who die unexpectedly have little time for good-byes, no time to attend to unfinished business, or to review their life's story and purpose. But those individuals living with a life-threatening illness encounter many lonely moments when there is time to ponder the meaning and purpose of their lives. What has been accomplished and what has not? Is there something pressing that has been left undone? What has my life been about, and what do I leave behind? Will anyone remember me?

Sometimes these questions and the search for their answers lead to the "redirection" that author Bernie Siegel, M.D., refers to in the quotation that began this chapter. Stories, even the personal stories of our lives, need endings in order to feel complete or resolved, and some individuals choose to take charge and write their own closing chapter. Mr. Schmidt's lesson for all of us is that life is not over until it is over, and amazing things can be accomplished during the ending of a life. Until the very end of life, people can surprise us; they can even surprise themselves. Of course, not everyone facing death can or will take advantage of this opportunity to complete unfinished business or redirect their life story.

TIME IS PRECIOUS

Mother Teresa is credited with having taught us that "We cannot do great things on this earth. We can only do small things with great love." However, even small acts can have great impact, whether on our immediate family or a sea of strangers. Less than three months before he died, Mr. Schmidt met a grandchild he might otherwise never have known, and was able to let his previously abandoned daughter know that she had not been forgotten. This father and daughter were given the precious opportunity to say both hello and good-bye.

During the ending of life, there is a window of opportunity for amazing growth, great love, meaningful spiritual reconciliation, and everlasting gifts to others.

Mr. Schmidt's story reflects a powerful and inspiring paradox. During times of such sadness, loss, possible suffering, and so many endings, there are sometimes truly beautiful glimmers of beginnings and awakenings. Loved ones may get the chance to say words they have long needed to but been unable to say, and they may be heard in a very different way from what would have been possible under different circumstances.

The capacity of the human spirit to seek closure and resolution even under dire circumstances is an inspiring sight to behold. So with each heartbreaking ending, there is also an opportunity to say that last good-bye in a loving and meaningful way.

LIFE WITH CANCER

Time, even time spent living with cancer, can be precious. A more contemporary example than Mr. Schmidt is singer-songwriter David M. Bailey. According to his website (www .davidmbailey.com), David is the son of Presbyterian missionaries. As a young man he played guitar, joined some bands, and started writing some songs. But adulthood and marriage led to a more stable career in corporate America.

In 1997, David was diagnosed with a glioblastoma brain tumor and given six months to live. With seemingly little to lose, David quit his mainstream career and starting writing songs again. Since 1997, he has released approximately eighteen albums of predominantly Christian folk/rock music filled with words of hope and inspiration. David is now a twelve-year cancer survivor and has spent these past twelve years writing, singing, and sharing songs of hope, faith, and survivorship for audiences worldwide.

In late 2008, David was diagnosed with a recurrence of his tumor and is now undergoing additional treatment. Despite this new round of adversity, he maintains an impressively active touring and recording schedule. David recently wrote the words below in reference to this new chapter in his journey of life with cancer.

> *So things are not as good as I wish they were*
> *But they ain't as bad as I know they could get*
> *So the monster in my head chose to recur*
> *I wonder if it thought I would forget*
>
> *So, yeah, things could be better, but I say take them as they are*
> *Pretty soon they'll be so good we'll wonder how we got so far*

And if you stumble on a bump or two somewhere down the line
I guarantee it will not help if all you do is whine
Just let it be another chance to learn to love the time
Sure, things could be better, but they've never been so fine.
At least we're free to choose our response and for today that's mine
I don't always remember that but trust me, I am trying
And if the sun comes up again, I'll call it a sign
What could be better already is; sing hallelujah just one more time.

—DAVID BAILEY, *singer, songwriter, cancer survivor*
(www.davidmbailey.com)

David Bailey listened to the warning shot of a life-threatening illness and seemingly decided his remaining time was too precious to waste on anything less than his life's passion and calling. Many others have benefited from his decision to do so. One of David's customary "mantras" is hidden within the poem above. It is *"love the time."* I think of it as his theme song, and I wish it to be all of ours as well.

Chapter Three

IN TECHNICOLOR

There are only two ways to live your life.
One is as though nothing is a miracle.
The other is as though everything is a miracle.

—ALBERT EINSTEIN

IN TECHNICOLOR

I have now spent more than thirty years working with individuals who have unexpectedly faced a life-threatening illness. Many of my patients have spontaneously commented that this face-to-face confrontation with their own mortality has allowed them to see the world in Technicolor instead of black and white. They have often wryly commented, "Why did it take dying to make me appreciate living?"

Why, indeed? Is it human nature to take most things for granted and then, only when we are about to lose something, realize how much we want it? Is it simply that we want what we can't have? Young children have this wonderful tendency to notice and wonder about everything. I remember my own young ones asking such questions as "Why is the sky blue?" and "Why do the leaves turn red and yellow instead of pink and purple?" (I also remember being embarrassed because I didn't know the answers to these seemingly simple questions.) But I also noticed that my children seemed much more in touch with and curious about the simple miracles of everyday life than I was. Do we start out more aware and appreciative of the world around us and then lose that capacity as the realities and responsibilities of adult life overcome us?

In Mitch Albom's touchingly beautiful book *Tuesdays with Morrie*, dying college professor Morrie Schwartz tries to explain to his former student that if you "learn how to die, then you learn how to live." According to Morrie, we all know that we're going to die, but we live as if we have forever, and thus get lost in the less-than-significant details of daily life. It is as if we're living on automatic pilot. Instead, we should accept and prepare for the inescapable time limitations of our life span. Then we would be more actively involved in living each day and more focused on what is truly important. I tend to agree with Morrie.

Living our lives in Technicolor instead of black and white requires a shift in perspective. There is clearly a fundamental difference between merely existing and thankfully embracing each new day. There is also a difference between approaching each new day as if it were one big, burdensome to-do list versus imbuing each day with a renewed sense of goal-driven meaning, mission, and purpose. Why and how do some of us just live our lives whereas others celebrate theirs? And is there a way that we might all learn to live our lives more fully and genuinely, without confronting a life-threatening illness or some other tragedy?

The key ingredients of this altered life view may include both a renewed sense of appreciation for what is, and a sharper vision of what is truly important.

TEMPORARY APPRECIATION

Many years ago, I took an art class with my then school-age son. The class took place over several weeks on Saturday afternoons and was focused on using charcoal to sketch patterns of light and dark. Neither my son nor I had any particular artistic inclinations, but the point of this parental exercise was to give us both several hours of quiet time to just be together and perhaps chat. So for several weeks we sat outside and looked intently at the patterns of sunlight and shadow that defined the big old tree we were both ineptly trying to replicate on our sketch pads, and we talked.

I remember this as a nice time. I also remember the unexpected aftermath of this artistic venture. For about a month after this exercise in light/dark concentration, I saw the world around me as if it were a bright collage of sunlight and shadows. It was truly beautiful. I knew even then that this enhanced ability to truly see and appreciate the world around me would gradually fade. And it did, although every once in a while as I'm driving to work, all of a sudden I forget what I'm thinking about and "see" a particularly beautiful tree in its full fall majesty or appreciate how the sunlight is gently awakening the new day, and I'm grateful for the reminder of the beauty all around me.

But you don't need to take an art class to visit this land of temporary appreciation. Those who go away on prolonged business trips often come home with a greater awareness of the comforts and conveniences of their own homes. Several of the young medical residents whom I teach make mission trips to third-world countries to provide much-needed health care. For several weeks after these young doctors return to the States, they are so very grateful for the daily niceties such as hot showers, comfortable bed linens, and wood versus dirt floors, which many of us might easily take for granted. Or how about the early stages of a new relationship, when everything the other person does is endearing or charming in some way?

A simple exercise might help us all to cultivate a capacity to better appreciate the world and the special people around us. Try to end each day by spending several minutes writing down three to five things that you appreciate or are grateful for about your day. These items can be very big and meaningful but also could be very small and meaningful. A beautiful sunset, a child's uninhibited laughter, or a stranger's friendly smile or gesture are all gifts to be absorbed and noted. For some of my patients, a phone conversation with a dear friend or the fact that the pain wasn't too bad that day would also make the list.

The trick of this deceptively simple assignment is that it helps us to pay more attention and to be more aware of life's big and small blessings. Taking the time to actually write down your three to five items of gratitude seems to be far more effective than just thinking those brief appreciative thoughts in your head. Hopefully, after several weeks or months of disciplining yourself to acknowledge life's blessings in writing on a daily basis, you will find yourself in a more positive, appreciative place.

SETTING PRIORITIES

How many of us, at this moment, would have no regrets about how we have lived our lives and what we have or have not accomplished? How many of us would feel that we have lived almost every day of our lives fully and genuinely? In order to eventually look back with few regrets, we need to develop a sense of true clarity about our life priorities. What is most important to me? Who is most important to me? What will I feel most bad about if I never get it done? What kind of person do I want to be? How do I want to be remembered? To live life genuinely and fully implies that we know the answers to these and many other similar questions. Realistically, most of us are too busy and distracted by life's incessant, daily details to look at this big existential picture.

But we do get occasional glimpses of this larger life view. When we fantasize about winning the lottery and mentally plan out how we'd like to spend our life-altering winnings, only to be rudely interrupted when someone else has the nerve to win our hoped-for pot of gold, we are making some internal statement about priorities. The common T-shirt slogan SHE WHO HAS THE MOST TOYS WINS may be a valid reflection of our fast-paced, consumer-oriented culture, but is it true?

In classes for health-care professionals, we often introduce the sessions on End of Life Issues with an exercise that goes something like this: If you knew for sure that you had twenty-five more years to live, what would you be sure to do or not do? How about if you had only fifteen years left to live, what would change? What about only ten more years to live or, worse yet, only five more years? And lastly, if you had only one more year to live, how would you spend that precious last year? What tasks or life commitments would definitely not be on the last year's to-do list? Now look back at all of your responses. Are there any patterns that suggest your particular life's priorities or passions? Are you currently doing any of the things that you've indicated are so important to you? And if not, why not—what are you waiting for?

So-called midlife crises or reactions are also about our awakening sense of pending time constraints. The resulting "Is this all there is?" frustration can lead to either meaningful or not-so-meaningful life alterations. The effectiveness of individual

solutions to midlife reminders that one is getting older seem
to vary considerably. The proverbial red sports car may help
one feel younger or more attractive, but it is less likely to
make anyone's life more meaningful.

What will make my life meaningful and joyful at the same
time? The lesson in this chapter is that we should all take the
time to periodically ask this question, even if we haven't yet fig-
ured out the answer.

WAKE-UP CALLS

Serious illness and loss of a spouse are two of the harsher calls
to a larger reality. The first presses you to decide, perhaps
quickly, how to best spend your remaining time here on earth.
The latter forces you to reinvent yourself in ways that you had
neither imagined, planned for, nor desired. These intimidating
time constraints or life changes can lead to immobility, bitterness, and confusion or to personal clarity and reprioritization.

Nell was a sixty-four-year-old widow of a well-known pe-
diatrician. She was slightly overweight and dressed neatly, but
not necessarily becomingly, during our first office visit. She wore
a long, girlish haircut, and her distinctively blue eyes looked
sad. Nell had been widowed two years earlier. Her physician-
husband had been a diabetic who unfortunately spent the last
several years of his life suffering many of the complications of
his chronic illness. Nell and her late husband had one living
adult child, a son, who had relocated several states away three
years prior to our first meeting. The couple had lost another
child, a daughter, to leukemia many years earlier. Financially,
Nell was comfortably provided for. Emotionally, she was lost
and immobilized.

During our first session, Nell reported that she had gone

through the first year of widowhood in a daze of exhaustion. She had spent the last six months of her spouse's prolonged illness caring for him literally day and night. After the funeral, she pretty much took to bed and caught up on much-needed sleep while courting emotional oblivion.

During the second year of widowhood, Nell drifted aimlessly. "All my life, I've been a wife and mother. I don't know how to be anything else. I don't know if I want to be anything else. I feel so lost and so stuck. I have no purpose. I'm not contributing anything. I'm just wasting time, but I don't know what to do about it. I know that I should be doing something, but I don't know what that is, and I don't know how to figure it out. So that's why I'm here."

Nell and her husband had had a reasonably good relationship. Before marriage, Nell had studied nursing but had worked only briefly before meeting her physician-husband-to-be. His career and more extroverted personality had driven both their lifestyle and social existence. Nell had a fine relationship with her adult son, but he was busy with his own career, and visits between mother and son were infrequent. Nell had good neighbors and friends, but they too had busy, seemingly fulfilled, lives. Nell wasn't truly alone, but she was lonely.

Clinically, I didn't think that Nell was depressed per se. She was certainly unhappy and understandably still grieving, along with struggling to adjust to a new, uncertain chapter in her life. At the close of our first session, I asked Nell to reflect on any possible activities that she might enjoy or find fulfilling in some way. Nell was quiet for several minutes, but then shrugged her shoulders in sad frustration, replying, "I just don't know." I smiled and responded, "Then you'll just have to relax and enjoy the process of discovering them." I then rattled off a list of potential activities or interests to consider. Some of the items on my list were plausible (a knitting club, a book-reading group, line-dancing lessons, a water-aerobics class, joining a singles travel club) and other items on my list were a bit far-fetched (mountain climbing, juggling classes, or roller-blading). For the first time, Nell smiled. We had reframed an overwhelming task as a playful adventure.

Over the next several months, Nell tried out various activities. Some she liked; others she didn't. It didn't matter. All that mattered was her willingness to try and to trust herself to figure it out as she went along. The more things she tried, the more her self-confidence and self-awareness grew. Nell was slowly redefining herself, reinventing her life, and finding the whole journey more than a bit interesting.

Eventually certain patterns became clear. Nell had cared for her leukemic daughter during her prolonged illness, and many years later had been caregiver to her ailing husband. Nell liked giving, taking care of people, and feeling useful. Eventually Nell and her local Rotary Club found each other. Nell met many like-minded humanitarian individuals and began traveling abroad to learn about and provide aid in underserved countries.

Nell and I recently ran into each other at a local fund-raising event. She looked fit and healthy. Her girlish haircut had been traded in for a shorter, more confident style. Her blue eyes glowed with energy and excitement as she described the next upcoming Rotary trip to Africa. Nell had "woken up" and rediscovered who she was and who she could be.

Any number of other life transitions may lead us to stop, step back, and try to figure out who we are and who we want to be. The awesome responsibility of becoming or being a parent often awakens us to a need to be clear about what we truly believe, value, and want to teach our children. An old friend of mine, after adopting a much-wanted child, poignantly commented, "I can't imagine what I ever thought was important before this." Being responsible for another human being is a definite invitation to a life-altering shift in perspective.

Other opportunities for reprioritization and self-reflection are more bittersweet. Marital separation or divorce, retirement, and the empty-nest phase of family life all invite us to redefine or reinvent ourselves in meaningful ways. "What's important to me now?" can be a challenging question to ask. But the answer can serve as a much-needed flashlight in the dark.

My friend Melissa and I went to graduate school together. The toils and torments of grad school were so much more palatable because of the joys of our shared friendship. We both joined the same university faculty and taught together that first year after grad school. But then life, family moves, and careers intervened, and we lost touch for more than twenty years.

A year ago we rediscovered each other. Once again we are living in the same city. During our twenty-year hiatus Melissa had become a breast cancer survivor, and I had experienced several surgeries. We are older and wiser and more aware of how quickly life can change. We now talk on the phone every few days, and go on a cultural outing at least once a month, whether we need it or not. Each time we get together, we spend the first several minutes congratulating ourselves for making the effort and taking the time to be together. This time around, we will not just enjoy our friendship; we will celebrate it.

DON'T FORGET TO SAY "I LOVE YOU"

Years ago, while conducting a training session for hospice volunteers, an attractive middle-aged widow shared a brief but poignant story with me. She and her husband had a morning ritual of always saying "I love you" and kissing each other good-bye before he left for work. It had seemed like a nice way to start the day. Sadly, one fateful morning, the ritual was forsaken in the face of pressing time demands. Two hours later a policeman showed up at this gentle woman's door to inform her that her husband had been killed in a motor vehicle accident caused by another hurried commuter.

Her story touched me greatly and has stayed with me throughout the years. I end every phone conversation with my children by saying "I love you," just in case. They already know that I love them, but it never hurts to say it again. I want my beloved family members, my good friends, and my special colleagues all to know how important they are to me and how grateful I am that they are in my life. So I remind myself to take the time to tell them so. It's so easy to forget, but I try not to.

We should not leave unsaid the things that are most important to say.

My goal for each of my seriously ill patients is that they should find a way to live their remaining days as meaningfully and comfortably as possible. I would like their days to be filled with moments of vivid appreciation for what is or has been, versus what is about to be lost. I would like as many of them as possible to truly believe that their lives have served a purpose, and that they have done the best they could to live well. But that is my hope for all of us as well.

Chapter Four

GENEROSITY

*Grant that I may not so much seek to be consoled, as to console;
To be understood, as to understand; To be loved,
as to love; For it is in the giving that we receive . . .*

—*Prayer of* SAINT FRANCIS

SELFLESS ACTS

The human capacity to reach out to others without any expectation of personal reward or gain could be labeled generosity, altruism, or selflessness. But by any name, it's a wondrous sight to behold. I am always touched and impressed when I witness or read about selfless acts, particularly when they involve strangers. But I am truly awestruck when I observe altruism among those who are dying or grief-stricken.

From a psychological perspective, I don't think that we are born to be selfless, generous creatures. Quite the contrary: We come into this world wanting and needing to get our own needs met. And if we're lucky, we do. In fact, for some of us, becoming a parent is our first true introduction to the experience of putting someone else's needs consistently before our own. Some people do choose vocations that emphasize service over personal advancement. And others choose to make great and unplanned sacrifices for total strangers. An example of the latter would be those generous souls who sign up for organ donation. And then there are some truly amazing human beings who find the personal strength and compassion to reach out to others despite the overwhelming reality of their own suffering. I have been fortunate enough to meet some of these very special people.

MY FRIEND JIM

Let me tell you about my friend Jim. Jim was a family physician. We worked together, taught together, and cared for some shared patients together. Jim loved life, had a raucous laugh, and was a gifted teacher and diagnostician. Jim both intimidated and encouraged each of the young physicians he trained. He was their most honest critic and, at the same time, their most enthusiastic supporter. Jim was one of those big-personality people. If he was in the room, you knew it. On the surface, he was an unlikely candidate for model citizen. My friend Jim was a blunt man. He always said what he meant, and he wasted no time in trying to sugarcoat it. He used several choice swear words frequently and joyfully. In short, he was a character, but also a very good man.

A number of years ago, Jim was diagnosed with an aggressive lung cancer. We were all shocked. He had always seemed larger than life. Jim chose to continue teaching and sought health care at the very same institution where he taught. He sacrificed privacy for a greater good. He wanted to keep teaching all of us as long as he could. He requested that the very same residents who were his students provide his daily care when he easily could have received care from only the most experienced and credentialed physicians. When he was no longer strong enough to teach, Jim still attended our program's noontime lectures—in his pajamas. He was reminding all of his students and colleagues alike that street clothes, pajamas, or hospital gowns did not alter the essence of a human being. My friend chose not to go quietly into the night, and we all benefited from his courage.

But Jim's final lessons were not done. Shortly before he died, he started a scholarship program to aid young aspiring primary-care physicians who might require financial assistance in order to make their dreams of serving others come true. That scholarship program continues to this day and has provided relief to many struggling young medical students as they try to overcome the financial burdens of their extended medical educations.

SOARING SPIRITS

Dr. Randy Pausch's use of the all-too-brief time between his pancreatic cancer diagnosis and his untimely death is a more recent and truly inspirational example of altruism under fire. Randy understandably made a concerted effort to use his precious time to create a support network for his wife and a living legacy of memories for his young children. But shortly after receiving the devastating diagnosis of advanced pancreatic cancer, Randy also gave all of us *The Last Lecture*. In both the video and book version, Randy chose to share with family, friends, and strangers alike his poignant thoughts on how to live well, regardless of the circumstances. To this date, millions of Internet viewers and readers have been touched by Randy's generous and enthusiastic lesson.

Other public examples of true generosity include Cindy Lightner, who founded the organization MADD, Mothers Against Drunk Driving, after losing her own child to a drunk-driving accident. The TV show *America's Most Wanted* was created by John Walsh after the senseless murder of his own young son and is now part of a national effort to find missing children. Both of these remarkable individuals somehow managed not only to survive the unimaginable devastation of losing a child but also to find the strength, compassion, and energy to act on an altruistic desire to prevent others from experiencing similar tragedies.

A new friend of mine, Michele Neff Hernandez, is another example of this particular form of selflessness amidst personal suffering. Michele is a thirty-nine-year-old freelance writer and mother of three who lost her husband, Phil, in a tragic bicycle accident in late August 2005. Early in her widowhood, Michele struggled with the despair, turmoil, and confusion common to those acutely grieving, along with the added challenges of coping with a sudden, unexpected loss and the inherent isolation of being a younger widow. After all, Michele was only thirty-five years old when she lost Phil.

Although Michele benefited from a strong support network comprised of loving friends and family members, she found no one to talk to who truly understood the daily challenges of being a new widow. Painful questions such as "What do I do with my husband's wedding ring?" or "When should I give away his clothes?" remained unanswered. Michele decided that she needed to talk to other widows. So, intending to write a book on widowhood, she started to travel around the country interviewing widows of all ages and circumstances. Although that book is yet to be written, Michele was quickly appreciative of the potential support and empowerment available should these isolated groupings of widowed women come together. To this end, she founded Widows Bond (www.widowsbond.com), a free service that matches widows of similar demographics and circumstances for e-mail correspondence. Michele understood that when we choose to support others, we also help ourselves.

But my energetic friend was not done. She then became the executive director of Soaring Spirits Loss Foundation, a non-profit organization aimed at providing resources and support to those who have lost a loved one. This foundation connects those who serve grieving people with those in need. In July 2009, the Soaring Spirits Loss Foundation hosted its first National Conference on Widowhood. Widows from all over the country and the world met in San Diego, along with bereavement specialists from all over the country, and spent three amazing days teaching and learning from one another. I was fortunate to be one of the presenters at this conference, and it was a sight to behold. Thanks to the generous spirit and creative vision of one young widow, hundreds of bereaved people were brought together to provide comfort and support for one another; giving strength to others as they found their own.

EMPATHY

No man is an island, entire of itself: every man is a piece of the continent, a part of the main . . . any man's death diminishes me, because I am involved in mankind; and therefore never send to know for whom the bell tolls; it tolls for thee.

—John Donne

There are many other less public examples of those who have the remarkable capacity to turn personal tragedy into an opportunity to help others. Many of the hospice volunteers I have trained over the years are themselves widows or widowers.

These charitable human beings choose to support others who are confronting losses similar to their own instead of distancing themselves from any unnecessary exposure to serious illnesses and acute grief.

COMFORTING OTHERS

Marty is a sixty-seven-year-old retired banker. He is now gray-haired, but exudes a youthful energy and intelligence. Marty lost his wife, Jean, to ovarian cancer about six years ago. He has not remarried, but leads an active life with much of his time spent visiting his children and grandchildren. He is an avid golfer, takes classes at a local college just for fun, and regularly exercises at the local gym. Marty is also a hospice volunteer. He spends one to two days per week traveling to various homes and providing respite services to families caring for a dying loved one. No task is too small. Marty is happy to help out in any way that he can. He's also happy to just sit there and listen. He remembers how exhausting and isolating those last months were when Jean was dying at home.

I met Marty at one of the hospice volunteer training sessions that I periodically teach. He had contributed thoughtfully and helpfully to our class discussion, so I approached him after class to thank him for his comments. We grabbed a cup of coffee and chatted for a while. Marty indicated that he had been a hospice volunteer for about four years and that he looked forward to each new assignment.

Marty did admit that some of the time spent on hospice assignments was painful and brought back to the surface memories of his own experiences with a cancer-stricken spouse. But he added, "This is my chance to pay back those who helped me survive Jean's illness and death. This is also my opportunity to show to those who are just approaching the loss that I've survived, that they can do it too. It's worth a little discomfort to make a contribution like that, especially at my age."

If one of the aforementioned hospice volunteers hadn't experienced a cancer death, or if Marty hadn't lost a beloved spouse to ovarian cancer, would they have chosen to be hospice volunteers anyway? I don't know. But I do wonder if having experienced some particular form of suffering makes some people feel more connected and thus more concerned about others who are in the midst of similar struggles. I think so. This inclination to turn our own despair into an opportunity to comfort others reflects the best of our potential as human beings.

TWICE BLESSED

Perhaps in reaching out to comfort others,
we also find a way to comfort ourselves.

Giving to others is a very compassionate but also essentially therapeutic way to enhance our own personal sense of purpose and meaning. At some point in time, most of us yearn to feel that our lives have mattered and that we are appreciated in some way. This may be why selfless acts such as volunteerism can make us feel so much better about ourselves. I often suggest volunteer work as a possible strategy for those clients struggling with their sense of self-worth.

During their adolescent years, my son and daughter were each required by their father and me to participate in some form of community service or volunteer work. It was probably a lot to ask, considering the already pressing demands of their academic responsibilities as well as their various social and recreational activities. But this is one parenting strategy that I neither question nor regret.

My son, Jay, volunteered as an aide for our neighborhood after-school program. I would pick him up on my way home from work and quietly watch as my teenage son showed signs of the patient, loving father he is today. My daughter, Jen, fulfilled her commitment by spending time at a local children's rehabilitation facility—perhaps foreshadowing the challenging clinical work she would later do with troubled children and adolescents. Amid the confusion, temptations, and turmoil of adolescence, I believe that these volunteer experiences allowed my two children to hold on to some basic sense of their own purpose and self-worth.

In my city, the Race for the Cure is held rain or shine every Mother's Day. This is an annual fund-raising event for breast cancer. It is well publicized and, regardless of weather conditions, well attended. If you choose, you can wear a colored T-shirt indicating your status as a breast cancer survivor or as someone who is walking/running in support of another person who is living with or has succumbed to breast cancer. It tends to be both an exhilarating and emotional event. Families living with breast cancer in their midst run together. Children of mothers lost to this prevalent disease run holding hands with tears in their eyes. Sisters, aunts, daughters all touched by the genetic threat of this disease run in the name of a relative lost but also for all the other unrelated "sisters" out there who will hopefully be cured of or never experience this heartbreaking illness. Life-threatening illness teaches us the limits of our control. Volunteerism reminds us that there is always something that we can do.

> *The quality of mercy is not strain'd*
> *It droppeth as the gentle rain from heaven*
> *Upon the place beneath: it is twice bless'd.*
> *It blesseth him that gives and him that takes.*
>
> —WILLIAM SHAKESPEARE

Chapter Five

HOPE AND FAITH

Time is more precious than silver
Love is more precious than gold
Grace is more precious than diamonds
Beautiful, brilliant and bold.

Hope is more precious than sunshine
Faith is more precious than rain
Friends are more precious than passion
Walking with you through your pain.

—DAVID BAILEY, *songwriter, singer,*
cancer survivor (www.davidmbailey.com)

A BALANCING ACT

The balancing act of acknowledging the strong possibility of your life nearing its end and yet still staying engaged and very much alive is a daunting task. Some of my patients have performed this feat very publicly, and others have done so quietly but no less impressively. On many occasions, I have been involved in therapeutic conversations where both a funeral and the next vacation were simultaneously discussed. Many of my patients schedule their birthday celebrations around their chemotherapy treatments. The capacity of these clients to fight off despair and remain actively among the living never ceases to amaze and inspire me. This is not denial. This is a decision to make the best of whatever is possible, despite dire circumstances.

In order to accomplish this truly death-defying balancing act, one has to find a way to say to oneself and others, "This illness may ultimately win the battle for my life, but not today. Today I choose life. I am not dying with this illness; I am living with it, and I want to live well. So let's talk about what I want to do or accomplish today." The therapeutic mantra for this challenging but worthwhile balancing act is:

Hope for the best, but prepare for the worst.

VACATION PHOTOS

Teresa was sixty-two years old and loved to travel. She was the oldest daughter of a large extended Italian family and had never married. Her three younger sisters were married and all lived nearby. Teresa had been an elementary school teacher for more than twenty-five years, and upon retirement she chose to work part-time at a local travel agency. When she wasn't helping others plan their fantasy vacations, she was a devoted aunt to a handful of nieces and nephews. Teresa also maintained close ties with three girlfriends from high school.

Teresa dutifully took a one-week vacation every year. She had traveled all over the United States and loved each and every trip. But she had never gone abroad. More important, she had never been to Italy. Going to visit her family's homeland was Teresa's longed-for dream vacation. But for one reason or another (a family wedding here, a nephew's birthday party there), this special trip was put off from one year to the next. "I can always go to Italy next year," she'd say.

In the fall of 2007, Teresa was diagnosed with lung cancer. Ironically, although a one-pack-a-day smoker since age seventeen, Teresa had quit smoking one year earlier due to a recurrent cough. When Teresa met with her oncologist, he outlined a several-month course of chemotherapy infusions and then radiation treatments. Teresa asked only one question, "Could I possibly make a trip to Italy before we start? I've wanted to go there all my life, and I'm afraid that I'll be too sick afterward and may not ever get there." The oncologist paused for only a second before he agreed. He understood the importance of dreams to loving life and staying alive.

Next Teresa called her three best girlfriends and told them about her fairly spontaneous travel plans. Blessedly, each of these three women was able to drop everything, and two weeks later the foursome left for their ten-day excursion through northern Italy. Teresa came home ready to enter the oncologic battlefield. She brought her Italian vacation photographs with her every treatment day. Her body fought its cancer while her imagination revisited the splendors of Italy.

Today, Teresa is still alive and still working at the travel agency when she is not traveling herself or playing aunt to a growing plethora of youngsters. So far her cancer is in remission. But Teresa isn't taking any chances; she's planned another trip to Italy just in case. Teresa doesn't postpone her dreams anymore.

THE TRAJECTORY OF HOPE

Years ago, it was thought that as soon as an individual learned of his or her terminal prognosis, all personal hope was lost. That is not necessarily so. During a life-threatening illness, what one hopes for shifts over time, yet most patients manage to remain hopeful in some way. Early on, most of us might be inclined to hope that our recently experienced pain or weight loss really isn't anything serious. We might also hope that the doctor will have a quick and easy solution for our current ills. Once we've been told that we have a serious illness, we might hope that it will respond quickly to treatment or that the treatment itself will not be too difficult.

Later on, if our illness does not respond well to the treatment, our hopes will shift again. At this point in time, one's hopes become much more specific to the person involved in the illness experience. Many of us will hope for sufficient pain control, or enough time left to make it to our daughter's wedding. Others will hope for time to get their affairs in order, or one last special visit with their grandchildren. And still others will hope for some semblance of retained dignity and self-control. Ultimately, this trajectory of hope amidst serious illness becomes a very personal journey.

CHERISHING THE MOMENTS

Carrie was a petite, slender woman in her early fifties. Her makeup was understated but skillfully applied. Her posture was regal, and her attire was casually elegant. In short, Carrie was a gracious, attractive, intelligent woman, married to an affluent and influential man. Carrie and her husband were a "power couple" in their community. Both were active contributors and organizers of many local and national humanitarian efforts. Carrie also had a devastatingly aggressive lung cancer.

Carrie was a very private person, living a very public life. During the nine months that we worked together, Carrie never shared with her family that she was seeing a therapist. Therapy was her personal time and her private battleground. She chose to fight her periodic bouts of anxiety and depression privately. Publicly, she remained active and involved in both family life and her many community commitments. Despite this sharp demarcation of private versus public persona, Carrie was blessed with a large network of truly caring friends and a close, supportive family.

Initially, Carrie's hopes were, predictably, that her cancer would respond to its fairly aggressive treatment. After many treatment failures and much physical distress, this very stoic woman shifted her hope from that of cure to a desire to "stay ahead" of the cancer. In short, she wanted to keep living life on her terms, despite the cancer. I can only imagine the energy it took, to be so sick and yet to remain so active and involved in everyday life. For Carrie, staying in control of her daily schedule was the operational definition of independence.

During this time period, as the cancer defeated one aggressive treatment after another and insidiously ravaged her body, Carrie remained not just active, but truly engaged in her life. She found things to hope for and look forward to. She treasured each and every moment with her children and grandchildren. Carrie had a lovely smile: It lit up the therapy room. She would begin every therapy session sharing moments of appreciation and joy before discussing her most recent illness experience. Carrie knew how to hope and how to cherish the moment.

REALISTIC VERSUS UNREALISTIC HOPES

Eventually, Carrie's hopes to remain in total control of her public persona and her demanding daily schedule became increasingly unrealistic. And so this strong, brave woman accepted this new reality and redefined independence as the hope that she would remain true to her values and priorities, even as her daily commitments and public appearances diminished. Committee memberships were vacated and speaking engagements were canceled, but contributions to important causes were secured, and times with close friends and family members were treasured. This last shift in her personal journey of hope was an important one. I believe that it allowed Carrie more peace toward the end of her life than she might have had otherwise.

Carrie continued to seek second opinions as long as she was physically able. She took part in several new and experimental treatment protocols. But in doing so, Carrie never denied the seriousness of her illness or its inevitable outcome. Carrie just chose to live life as fully as she could, and on her own terms, for as long as she could. Carrie balanced the realities of her progressing illness with the life priorities that defined who she was and would always be.

Successfully hoping for the best but preparing for the worst implies a capacity to distinguish realistic hopes from those that are unrealistic.

This can be easier said than done. Hope needs to be reconciled with the realities of each individual's illness and response (or non-response) to treatment over time. Failure to do so can lead to either missed treatment opportunities or prolonged periods of invasive but ultimately futile interventions. If one is unrealistically fearful and pessimistic, viable and potentially helpful treatment options may be discounted. If one is prematurely pessimistic, precious time may be spent anxiously waiting for "doomsday" instead of enjoying the moments at hand. Periodically, at the hospital we will encounter a patient who has delayed seeking needed treatment for many months, inevitably resulting in a poorer treatment response than might have otherwise occurred. These situations are particularly sad, because it seems that the futile attempt to avoid reality has simply compounded the individual's suffering instead of relieving it.

Conversely, if one is unrealistically optimistic and unable to accept the realities of a disease's progression, then the decision to shift from aggressive treatments to comfort measures may be delayed, leading to unnecessary medical expenses and more importantly, prolonged personal suffering. Denial of an illness's seriousness can also seriously handicap an individual or family's opportunity to seek resolution or attend to unfinished business. Physicians and therapists alike need to gently and respectfully support this process of routinely realigning the internal world of personal hope with the shifting external realities of a disease.

FINDING OUR OWN ANSWERS

For some, spirituality and hope are inextricably tied together, but this is not so for others. For some, faith-based inclinations are very specific and fixed, while for others these concepts are either absent, ambivalent, or vague and nebulous. A life-threatening illness or loss of a loved one may initiate a spiritual crisis, or else faith may be a source of great comfort during trying times. At the end of life, people will reconcile their own beliefs in their own way. In dying, as in living, we each must find our own answers. So faith, like hope, is a personal journey.

When you come to the edge of all the light you have known and are about to step out into the darkness, Faith is knowing one of two

things will happen . . . There will be something to stand on or you
will be taught how to fly.

—AUTHOR UNKNOWN

Bill was a fifty-eight-year-old salesman. He was a big, powerful man. He could be tough and intimidating, but also congenial
and generous. Bill loved life. He was an active and physical man.
Bill had been force-fed religion as a child, so as an adult he exer-
cised the privilege of rigidly rejecting anything religious. He
was a self-made man, and that was what he believed in.

In the winter of 1987, Bill, a long-term smoker and chronic
cougher, woke up and vomited blood. He was rushed to the
hospital and, in a matter of days, was diagnosed with lung cancer, had surgery to remove his diseased lung, and was placed
on a respirator. With little warning, life had changed drastically for Bill, his wife, and his grown daughter.

From the winter of 1987 until the spring of 1988, Bill lived
in a series of intensive-care or rehabilitation hospital rooms.
For much of this time, he was on a respirator and unable to talk.
However, being unable to talk didn't stop Bill from throwing a
number of well-intentioned pastors out of his various hospital
rooms. Bill's body had shrunk from an impressive 220 pounds
to a mere 140, but his determination to reject spiritual intervention was as strong as ever.

Tragically, only one month after finally returning home,
Bill became jaundiced and was subsequently diagnosed with a
second cancer. It was pancreatic cancer this time. Despite radiation treatments, this new cancer spread, and several months
later, Bill was placed on home hospice care. Bill's continued
decision to exclude religion from his life was a source of much

upset for his wife and daughter. They were concerned that Bill
would never find the peace that he deserved without some
form of spiritual reconciliation. And so, one more pastor was
introduced into the mix. His name was Frank, and he had been
a businessman in his pre-pastoral life. Frank started to visit
Bill's home, and they talked business, not religion. Clearly
Frank was a wise and patient man. He understood that Bill's
journey was his own.

MAKING PEACE

Bill and Frank became two men who enjoyed and respected
each other. Frank became someone Bill trusted. Gently, religion
was introduced into their now regular conversations. Shortly
before Bill died, Frank took a chance and brought communion
to the home. Bill surprised everyone present. He cried, and
shared that it had been more than thirty years since he had received communion, because he hadn't felt that he was worthy.
Several days later, Frank returned with several church elders,
and during a brief but touching bedside ceremony, Bill was officially entered into the church of his choosing. For Bill, spiritual reconciliation meant making peace with himself, not just
his God.

FAMILY DILEMMAS

Many family members like Bill's worry about the spiritual well-
being of their loved ones who are ill. A good friend of mine,
whose father is rapidly failing from a combination of congestive
heart failure and dementia, anguishes over her father's lack of
visible spiritual acceptance. She is convinced, based on her own
religious beliefs, that he will die without peace and will also

never be reunited with her mother and other deceased loved ones. My friend loves her father dearly, and this quandary frequently brings her to tears. She somehow feels responsible for her father's religious conversion, and therefore at fault if it does not occur in time. I have encouraged my friend to trust her God and her father to find the resolution to this seeming impasse. After all, no one person can be in charge of another's inner spiritual life or lack thereof. Additionally, some spiritual reconciliations are quite visible, whereas others are not. And again, perhaps some are needed and others are not.

ONE LAST HURDLE

Gladys was eighty-six years old, and she was having trouble dying. Gladys had suffered multiple strokes, which had left her bedridden and often quite confused. She remained in this compromised state for more than a year. Finally, Gladys contracted a viral infection that her weakened body could not fight off, and within several days she slipped into a coma. Until the last week of her life, Gladys's husband, Jerry, had been her sole caregiver. Jerry had refused any outside assistance. He would explain, "She has been mine since we were fifteen years old. This is my responsibility. And she would do the same for me if our situations were reversed."

Gladys and Jerry had met and fallen in love when they were both fifteen years old. They had been inseparable ever since. They had married in their early twenties, despite considerable family resistance. The objection stemmed from the differences in their respective religious upbringings. Gladys had been raised Catholic, and Jerry's family was Jewish. In order to maintain a semblance of peace within their two families, this loving couple agreed to raise their children in a nondenominational home, thus avoiding choosing one religion over the other. The decision to sacrifice the outward practice of a childhood faith was harder for Gladys than it was for Jerry. Nuns had schooled her, and her faith-based belief system was literal and strongly rooted. But Gladys knew she was meant to spend her life with this particular man. Jerry's beliefs were less specific and more nebulous. It was his love for Gladys that was simplistically clear.

Despite these notable obstacles, Gladys and Jerry were happily married for almost sixty years. Their children were educated about both religions and were encouraged to choose their own faith-based pathway as they reached adulthood. But one last hurdle remained. During the last week of Gladys's life, she was at home, cared for by a home hospice team and surrounded by her devoted husband, her grown children, and her grandchildren. But for seven days and nights, despite her frail condition, Gladys continued to struggle. She seemed unwilling or unable to die.

Finally, her daughter suggested that perhaps a priest should be called in to perform the last rites. Jerry initially declined, saying that after all these years he didn't think that the Catholic sacrament would be necessary. Certainly, Gladys should be at peace. She was, after all, a good woman and had been a wonderful wife and mother. The daughter gently persisted, explaining that as a schoolgirl, her mother would have been taught about the importance of this final holy ritual as a needed preparation before entry to heaven.

Jerry reluctantly acquiesced and a local priest was called to the home. Gladys was forgiven and blessed by this representative of her childhood faith. As soon as the blessing was completed, Gladys's breathing slowed and her face relaxed into a lovely, peaceful *Mona Lisa* of a smile. And then this good woman's life was finally over. Regardless of outward appearances, the rituals of Gladys's faith were a strong part of her life and a necessary ingredient to her dying.

Carrie's, Bill's, and Gladys's stories are about the very personal journeys of three very different people as they confronted a life-threatening disease. Carrie's story emphasizes the role of realistic but shifting hopes. Bill's ordeal speaks to the importance of personal faith and making peace. Gladys's final moments speak to the shared powers of love and faith, and the importance of respecting others' beliefs regardless of one's own. Each of these special individuals found ways to be true to themselves despite the significant challenges of their respective illnesses or complicated family dynamics.

> *Perhaps the rest of us shouldn't wait for a serious*
> *illness to pursue our own personal journeys*
> *of hopes, dreams, and faith.*

Chapter Six

ACCEPTANCE

The Serenity Prayer

*God grant me the serenity
to accept the things I cannot change;
courage to change the things I can;
and wisdom to know the difference.*

—REINHOLD NIEBUHR

In her first book, *On Death and Dying,* Dr. Kübler-Ross proposed five "stages" of dying. The first four stages were Denial, Anger, Bargaining, and Depression. The last of the five stages was called Acceptance, and so it was initially thought that the only so-called good or appropriate death was the one in which a patient peacefully accepted his or her fate. Clinical experience has taught many of us that these five emotional states are not actually consecutive steps to be climbed per se: They are merely fairly common patterns of emotional response that terminally ill patients demonstrate from time to time.

Some of us will quietly accept our life's end, while others of us will fight fiercely. Some of us will calmly discuss the realities of our fateful illness; others will bemoan or even deny their fate until the bitter end. Some people, particularly after a long illness, seem to almost welcome the ending of their and their family's suffering, whereas others are terribly frightened about what lies ahead. Over the course of a terminal illness, most individuals will experience all of the above. There will be moments of calmness and moments of restless anxiety; there will be fear, hopefulness, and periods of fleeting despair. The expectation that all of us will approach our dying with only Zen-like serenity is unrealistic at best.

DYING BRAVELY

An alternative idealized version of a good death involves the notion that we should "die bravely." It's hard to know exactly what dying bravely means, but for many of us raised on the popular media of the 1950s, '60s, or early '70s, it might mean approaching death in somewhat of a John Wayne–like (both barrels blazing) fashion. Other popular prototypes of machismo-infused bravery might include Clint Eastwood or the multiple reincarnations of James Bond. While these heroic, larger-than-life media performances make for good viewing, they do not represent accurate portrayals of real-life encounters with death or dying. These are one-dimensional explanations for far more complicated human reactions. After all, what does courage have to do with being afraid? Aren't we all entitled to be afraid of the unknown or of potential pain and suffering, much less the pending loss of all of our loved ones?

True courage is not the absence of fear, but the willingness to proceed in spite of it.

—AUTHOR UNKNOWN

QUIET COURAGE

Gerald was eighty-nine years old and suffering from a chronic lung condition (COPD) and Parkinson's disease. He had been widowed three years earlier, but until then had been his infirm wife's caretaker despite his own disabilities. Gerald lived alone but had three grown children; two sons who lived nearby, and a daughter who resided a day's plane trip away. He also had four grandchildren and one great-grandchild.

Gerald was a bright, well-spoken, older gentleman. His Parkinson's disorder had progressed to the point where he could no longer walk independently; the tremors in his hands made dressing and eating quite difficult; his speech was somewhat slurred and his once soft-spoken voice was now hoarse, but his mind was as sharp as ever. Gerald had accepted the progressive limitations of his diseased body with a quiet, flexible grace that had surprised his adult children. He had been a man some might have called rigid: He liked things just so. Everything in the refrigerator had its rightful place, and the houseplants were watered in a certain order. Perhaps Gerald's above-average intelligence allowed him to grasp that while some of life's details might be under his control, the realities of his illness were not. And so without complaint, he stoically accepted the inevitable indignities of his disease.

In addition to this marked stoicism, Gerald could also be depicted as a very traditional family man. His own father had been a talented athlete, but a self-centered person and an inconsistent provider. Gerald, on the other hand, while he shared his father's capacity for stubbornness, was a devoted spouse and a prudent financial provider for his own family of five. In short, Gerald was a good man who had worked hard, was modestly successful, and fortunate in love. His stoicism both as a sacrificing spousal caretaker and during the last stages of his own dying was a quiet kind of courage that could take your breath away if you were paying attention.

During the last forty-eight hours of his life, Gerald's gradually deteriorating physical status unexpectedly plummeted. Gerald's physician immediately called in home hospice, while Gerald's sons quickly came to the house and his out-of-state daughter hurriedly arranged her emergency travel details. Amidst all of this commotion, Gerald calmly struggled to breathe as he invested his last energies in preparing his grown children for his expected, yet somehow unexpectedly abrupt, demise. Gerald called his daughter and reassured her, "I don't want you to be upset if you don't make it here in time. There is nothing that I need for you to do for me right now, and there is nothing left unsaid between us. I am at peace, and these last several months of decline and suffering have simply affirmed for me that this is my time." Gerald then turned to his sons as they sat listening to the harsh sounds of his growing respiratory distress and told them, "You need to know that I am not in pain and I am no longer afraid. I have lived a good life. I have shared my life with my first love and best friend—your mother—which makes me luckier than most. And I can honestly say that I have no regrets."

After exerting his rapidly waning energy to take care of his children one last time, Gerald quietly whispered that he was tired and asked to be helped from his chair into his bed. As he lay down, he reminded his sons exactly where his eyeglasses should be placed on the nightstand table, and then closed his eyes and slipped into a coma. Hours later, surrounded by his three adult children, Gerald quietly let go of life and stopped breathing. I believe that by looking death unblinkingly in the eye and spending his last alert moments helping his children to accept and make peace with his death, Gerald exhibited a quiet but very John Wayne–like kind of courage. Of course, in this instance, I may be biased: You see, Gerald was my father.

Courage is also not an exclusively male domain. Nancy was a bubbly, blond-haired, pretty, and petite thirty-two-year-old mother of three young children. Nancy was a stay-at-home mom who had married her high school sweetheart. This blond, attractive young family lived in a lovely, sprawling home in a nice suburban neighborhood with good neighbors, friends, and family members nearby. It was a picket-fence kind of picture, except for the fact that Nancy had been living with and fighting leukemia ever since her early college years.

Nancy had experienced several relapses during her ten-year battle with leukemia. Each time she had become quite ill, but ultimately had responded well to treatment and had once again gone on living her otherwise satisfying life. This time was different. This time, there was no positive treatment response—just increasing fatigue, discomfort, and weight loss. Nancy's banker husband had taken a leave from work to help care for his seriously ill wife and three young children. And more recently, Nancy's mother had joined this sad household to help take care of both her ailing daughter and her daughter's young children.

The last several weeks of her life, Nancy spent more and more time in bed, often sedated for pain control. She spent less and less time with her children. This was a marked contrast from the active mother she had been only months before. Because the three children were very young (ages eighteen months, three, and four) and also surrounded by loving adults, they were confused by their mother's absenteeism but not necessarily frightened. They were allowed to periodically visit their mother in her bedroom when she was awake and not too tired or uncomfortable. But during these visits, they were guided to play quietly on the floor beside her sickbed in order to avoid inadvertently hurting or exhausting her with more physical play.

One particular evening after an especially uncomfortable day, Nancy called her mother and insisted that the children be brought to her room after bathtime so that she could read them their bedtime story. Nancy's mother protested, seeing the pain and fatigue in her daughter's eyes. But Nancy stubbornly repeated her request, "Please, Mom, this is important. I want to hold them in my arms and read them a bedtime story. I want to remember that feeling, and I want them to remember it too. I need to know that they will always remember that I loved them."

Nancy's husband and mother brought the three youngsters into their mother's sickroom and turned their heads away as this brave young mother grimaced while her three giggling children settled into her arms for one last time. The bedtime story was read, and Nancy's strained face relaxed for several moments as the children quieted in her embrace. With tears streaming down her face, Nancy kissed each of her little ones good night. She then requested the much-needed but postponed pain sedation and seemingly drifted off to sleep. Nancy never woke up the next morning. This brave woman had silently endured considerable pain in order to give her children the only type of good-bye that she had to offer and that they were old enough to experience.

So courage is not the sole domain of cowboys or special agents. We do not necessarily have to look to the television or movie screen for our heroes. Courage can involve years of quiet caretaking sacrifice or moments of silent suffering. Brave people come in all sizes, shapes, ages, and both genders. Courage or bravery does not require fearlessness, but it does require finding the strength and purpose to not run away but to face forward and do the best you can.

GRACE UNDER FIRE

One of the young physicians whom I teach recently told me about a death that he had just witnessed. His patient was a widowed, older woman approaching the end of her life, after a long respiratory illness. Over the last several months, she had been in and out of the hospital on multiple occasions. Each successive hospitalization had involved a series of unsuccessful interventions and much physical distress. She was, however, always accompanied by her very supportive and attentive grown children. Clearly, she was much beloved.

Shortly before her demise, this gentle woman experienced increasing respiratory distress. Once again, she was offered the option of ventilator support to ease her breathing. Calmly she refused intervention despite visible discomfort. She haltingly explained to her concerned young physician that she understood that the breathing machine would not correct her underlying terminal illness; it could only relieve some temporary suffering and prolong her life a bit longer. She felt it was time to let go, and she wanted to make that decision herself. Most important, she wanted to spare her children from having to make that heartbreaking decision for her.

My young physician friend and student was much more familiar and comfortable with addressing these end-of-life medical decisions with relatives, while the actual patients lay nonresponsive in their hospital beds. It was disconcerting to have this kind of conversation with the person doing the dying. His elderly patient died several hours later. When I asked him how her decision and death had made him feel, he replied,

"Humbled." I, too, am humbled by this woman's resolute acceptance of her inevitable fate. I am even more touched by her capacity to stay focused on sparing her children unnecessary distress despite her own not insignificant discomfort.

Susie was the five-year-old daughter of a very young and overwhelmed single mom. Despite her youth, Susie was the victim of a chronic illness. Susie, too, had been in and out of the hospital on multiple occasions, each time leaving a bit sicker than the time before. Susie was dying from liver failure. She was on the local children's hospital's list for a liver transplant, but of course, so were many other very sick children.

Susie's mother was unprepared for single parenthood in general, and certainly for the many tasks involved in caring for a seriously ill child. Susie and her young mom were pretty much alone in life, estranged from any family members and with no evident friends for support. Understandably, Susie's mom was pretty depressed. Day in and day out, this young, sad mother sat in her daughter's hospital room. She was so overwhelmed that she could barely move or talk; she just mutely sat in her daughter's darkened room. And so the hospital nursing staff "adopted" Susie and her mom. These kindhearted nurses took turns visiting, bringing in magazines for Mom and books for Susie. Meanwhile, I, too, visited daily and counseled Susie's mom as I simultaneously employed play therapy for my frightened young patient.

Eventually, our young mother's depressed state responded to these regular doses of support and companionship. She remained sad but became more animated, both with others and with Susie. Unfortunately, unlike her mother, Susie became sicker and gradually slipped into a coma. For forty-eight hours, Susie seemingly hovered somewhere between life and death. She was breathing unevenly, and every once in a while moaned ever so slightly. Her mother was constantly by her side, holding her hand and crying softly.

On the second night, the hospital chaplain and I finally convinced Susie's exhausted mother to take a nap in a nearby vacant room. I took her place at the bedside, holding Susie's hand, telling her not to be afraid. I felt compelled to reassure my young patient that although her mother was very sad, she was now strong enough to let Susie go. Susie's little body shuddered briefly; she gasped one final breath, and then all was quiet and still. My little patient's long ordeal was finally over. I don't know if she needed the reassurance that her mother would be all right. I don't know if this precious child actually waited for her mother to leave the room, to make it easier on the both of them. But at the time, it felt like this was true.

The elderly woman, the young single mother, and the little girl, along with Gerald and Nancy, all demonstrated grace under fire. They struggled, fought, and despaired, but ultimately they coped with the fateful realities before them as best they could. Despite their many differences, they all demonstrated great compassion and the capacity to think of others, even under the most adverse circumstances. They are some of my heroes. I don't know if they are best described as courageous, or simply capable of great love.

THE ILLUSION OF SELF-CONTROL

One of the major psychological challenges of coping with a terminal illness is the issue of losing control. Being in control means different things to different people, but most of us fear some version of losing control. We dread losing control of our bodies. We're uncomfortable with losing control of our emotions and our sense of personal privacy. We cringe at the notion of losing our independence and becoming increasingly dependent upon others.

HIGH EXPECTATIONS

Rita was a forty-five-year-old single woman, a nun, and a teacher who was highly intelligent and articulate. Rita had been diagnosed with breast cancer three years before our first therapy session. At that time, she had undergone a radical mastectomy and chemotherapy. Several months before our first visit, she had been diagnosed with pituitary cancer and had also undergone a second mastectomy, for a recurrence of her original breast cancer. Once again, Rita was undergoing chemotherapy. This time, she reluctantly sought out counseling to help her cope with the almost disabling panic attacks that she had reportedly been experiencing before each and every chemo treatment since her ordeal had begun three years prior.

Cognitively, Rita understood that her chemotherapy treatments were the needed medical tools to fight her advancing cancer. But emotionally, Rita could not stop herself from perceiving her now-weekly chemo infusions as dangerous poisons invading her body and causing a frightening cascade of unpleasant physical symptoms. She dreaded each and every treatment.

Anxiety symptoms, such as panic attacks, often run in families. So some of us are genetically more vulnerable to this experience than others. Rita came honestly by her predisposition to panic; she had a strong family history of anxiety disorders. Unfortunately, Rita was also caught in a vicious cycle. She dreaded becoming ill from her chemotherapy treatments, yet her high anxiety made this more likely. In fact, some days she was so agitated before her treatments that she actually started becoming nauseated before the infusion began. Being that she was an intelligent woman, this self-fulfilling paradox was not lost on her. In fact, it significantly increased her ongoing sense of disappointment in herself.

Rita had expected to maintain her composure at all times. She perceived these regular bouts of anxiety symptoms as personal failings and proof of innate weakness. She expected that as a member of a religious order, she would face all adversity with unquestioning faith and calm acceptance of whatever was to be. In her unrealistic self-scenario, emotions equaled loss of face and lack of self-control. These high expectations only added to Rita's already considerable suffering.

I believe that it took a good deal of bravery for Rita to seek out counseling. She worked hard at it for the brief time that we had together. She learned breathing and relaxation techniques to help her abort the worst of the panic symptoms, along with some of the inevitable side effects of her treatments. We also worked on the innate humaneness of all emotions, including fear. After all, someone capable of great compassion and faith might also expect to experience other strong emotions when the conditions warranted it.

Rita died several short months after we first met. I feel privileged to have known her, even for so brief a time. She was a truly special woman. She had taught, guided, and comforted many others during her shortened life. Rita died in the hospital, not totally unafraid, but respected, well loved, and surrounded by a roomful of her many Sisters and students.

There is no right way to die.

"A GOOD DEATH"

Many of my seriously ill clients eventually ask me, "What will my actual dying be like?" I usually answer, "Tell me what you'd like it to be like. And then let's see how close we can get to your image of how you'd like to die, whenever you eventually have to." Some people respond that they would hope to die at home surrounded by loved ones. Others respond that they envision dying in the hospital as privately and comfortably as possible. There is no right answer, only the opportunity to start to think about and plan for a meaningful personal ending.

Of course, implicit in this question is a more-than-fair request to be educated about what symptoms each individual is likely to experience as death draws close and what can be done to alleviate any distress. Some people never ask these questions, but many do. For those who do ask the questions, it may be scarier not to know. After all, some of us are planners and some of us are not. But I think that most people wonder and perhaps worry about the answers to these questions.

It is your physician's job to provide opportunities for you to ask these questions and then, when asked, to respond as honestly and humanely as possible. Even amid the nonnegotiable realities of dying, educated and informed patients may have opportunities to exert control in ways that are meaningful to themselves and/or their family members.

For example, Eric, a recent patient of mine, shared privately that he would much prefer to die at home, but was concerned about the level of physical suffering likely to occur during the terminal phase of his illness. He didn't want to expose his wife and children to traumatic memories that might haunt them forever. This man's ability to engage in this difficult initial conversation led to further conversations with his physicians. In this instance, Eric's distortions about uncontrolled suffering were corrected, and he did ultimately die at home. If the opportunity for this end-of-life conversation had been missed, those last priceless days of shared time between this young father and his wife and children might have been unnecessarily lost, and otherwise well-intentioned health-care providers might have inadvertently disregarded Eric's last wishes, priorities, and values.

Each of us has the opportunity to attempt to live our last weeks or days in a way that is consonant with our personal values, our lifestyles, our priorities, and our coping strategies. Life and death teach us that we are never in total control, but understanding that basic truth can free us to use our energies wisely and to make the most of the opportunities that we encounter along the way.

> *As in living, in our dying we may have another*
> *chance to decide what is most meaningful*
> *and important to us.*

PALLIATIVE CARE

From a medical perspective, end-of-life care refers explicitly to the health care that is provided during the final weeks or days of a person's life. Palliative care is a broader concept, encompassing any and all medical and supportive efforts employed to care for a seriously ill person and his or her family members once an illness is considered no longer responsive to curative treatments. I teach physicians how to provide compassionate palliative care, so I have given a good deal of thought to what we and our family members have a right to expect from our doctors once we are facing a life-threatening illness.

Medical care during a life-threatening illness should not be a dichotomous, all-or-nothing phenomenon. Patients should not perceive that their only health-care options are cure or comfort—or, even worse, cure or medical abandonment. So, I am somewhat taken aback when I occasionally hear a physician say to a terminally ill patient, "I'm so sorry, but I'm afraid that there is nothing else we can do for you." I'm tempted to interrupt with, "I don't believe that is true. You may be underestimating what you still have to offer during this difficult time. There is so much that you can still do for your patient and for their loved ones. Your job isn't done. You can still listen, support, and attend to your patient's concerns. You can still treat symptoms. You can still provide care and comfort, even when cure is no longer possible." But some physicians are so focused on saving lives or "fixing" their patients that they lose sight of other possible goals and meaningful contributions. Or perhaps their areas of training and expertise lie within the arenas of acute or emergent medical care instead of palliative care. Saving a patient's life is an amazing experience, but so is helping a patient to die comfortably, unafraid, and not alone.

OPTIMAL HEALTH CARE

Even the best physician cannot ultimately prevent all of his patients from dying. After all, we are all going to die at some point in time. So I would like for most physicians to be well trained in providing skillful and compassionate medical care, even when hope for cure is long gone. All of us have the right to be cared for by doctors who can provide optimal pain control, along with patient-specific and family-specific psychosocial support. The following list is not exhaustive, but it is a reasonable guideline for patients, their families, and their doctors regarding what optimal health care during a terminal illness might look like.

The Dying Patient's Bill of Rights

- I have the right to be treated as a living human being until I die.
- I have the right to maintain a sense of hopefulness, however changing its focus may be.
- I have the right to be cared for by those who can maintain a sense of hopefulness, however changing this might be.
- I have the right to express my feelings and emotions about my approaching death in my own way.
- I have the right to participate in decisions concerning my care.
- I have the right to expect continuing medical and nursing attention even though "cure" goals must be changed to "comfort" goals.
- I have the right to not die alone.
- I have the right to be free from pain.
- I have the right to have my questions answered honestly.
- I have the right to not be deceived.
- I have the right to have help from and for my family in accepting my death.
- I have the right to die in peace and with dignity.
- I have the right to retain my individuality and not to

be judged for my decisions, which may be contrary to the beliefs of others.

- I have the right to discuss and enlarge my religious and/or spiritual experiences, regardless of what they may mean to others.
- I have the right to expect that the sanctity of the human body will be respected after death.
- I have the right to be cared for by caring, sensitive, knowledgeable people who will attempt to understand my needs and will be able to gain some satisfaction in helping me face death.

This Bill of Rights was first created at a workshop conducted by Amelia J. Barbus, associate professor of nursing, Wayne State University, 1975. It was later reprinted in: Ferrell, B.R. and Coyle, N. "An Overview of Palliative Care Nursing." *American Journal of Nursing* 102 (May 2002): 26–31.

PART TWO

Loss and Grief:
A Family Perspective

Chapter Seven

GRIEF

*For everything there is a season . . .
a time to break down, and a time to build up;
a time to weep, and a time to laugh;
a time to mourn, and a time to dance. . . .*

—ECCLESIASTES 3:1–4

Grief is a normal and expected part of life. For all of us, there
will be a series of hellos and, eventually, good-byes. Grief is
such a common human experience that we have multiple words
in our everyday language to describe it. The word "loss" speaks
to the tangible and not-so-tangible things that we lose whenever someone important in our life dies. Every loss involves
multiple losses. We not only lose the deceased person, we lose
so many other pieces of the status quo that had been our life prior
to this loss. The word "bereaved" signifies that one has suffered a
loss. "Grief" is a small word, but it encompasses the overall reaction that we experience after a perceived loss. This grief reaction is physical and psychological, social and behavioral. This is
how we feel, think, and act after a loss. Finally the word
"mourning" depicts the psychological processes that we em-
ploy as we attempt to acclimate to a significant loss. The latter

is often called "grief work." This is how we try to survive, work through, and adapt to our loss.

However, despite the universality of the grief experience and the multiple words used to describe it, many individuals are unprepared for the profound impact and intensity of a bereavement experience. Recently widowed clients in my office often declare, "I'm afraid that I'm going crazy. I feel totally out of control. I've never experienced anything like this before, and I don't know what to do about it." But they are not crazy; they are grieving.

Grief is not just the prerogative of those who have recently lost a loved one; it is also a constant companion for the spouse watching his or her life partner gradually succumb to a life-threatening or debilitating illness. Grief is woven into the days of anxious parents as they watch their ill or disabled child struggle and fail to keep up with healthy siblings and peers. Likewise, grief is part of the ill person's daily adjustment to the changing limitations of his or her physical abilities coupled with the loss of a life without discomfort or doctor visits. So grief is part and parcel of many illness experiences, whether that illness ultimately leads to death or not. If you allow yourself to love, then at some point in time you will probably need to figure out how to grieve.

INDIVIDUAL REACTIONS

Grief is not a static state; it involves many different emotions over time. Grief doesn't have a set schedule. This life experience is not a race; the first one to reach the finish line doesn't necessarily win. How one expresses grief is highly individualized, and theoretically it is determined by many variables. For example, how any of us responds to a significant loss might depend on our own personality, along with our faith and cultural background. Our personal reactions might also be affected by the nature of our relationship with the deceased and how expected or unexpected the death was. Our unique reaction to loss might also be influenced by any prior experiences we have had with loss or death, along with any other concurrent stressors that may or may not be occurring in our lives. Lastly, our subjective experience with grief will be altered by the presence or absence of others to support and comfort us.

PREDICTABLE PHASES

Despite these individual variations on the theme, normal grief does seem to have several predictable, if overlapping, phases. Initially, most people will experience some level of shock, disbelief, or emotional numbness. The irreversible finality of never again seeing or being with someone who is and has been important in your life is simply too hard to grasp. During this phase, the new mourner's sentences often start with, "I can't believe . . ." Those newly bereaved often report the disconcerting sensation that they are stumbling around half asleep and expect to wake up at any moment to find this has all been some sort of nightmare.

In fact, many of my newly widowed clients dread waking up in the morning only to remember once again that a beloved spouse is truly gone. When a death has been sudden and thus unexpected, this early phase of disbelief can be expected to last a bit longer. But even if your loved one was ill for a very long time, it seems most of us will still experience some aspect of this initial shock and disbelief.

For example, even though nine long months of a prolonged illness had preceded her husband's death, one recent client spoke tearfully about how upset she was with herself, because on

multiple occasions she had picked up the phone to call her recently deceased husband about some minor household detail,
only to traumatically "remember" once again that he was no
longer there. As in the examples above, this early phase of shock
or emotional numbness tends to come and go a bit. It may provide the needed time to begin to approach an unthinkable and
unacceptable reality, but it can be disconcerting and challenging in its own right.

For better or worse, this beginning sensation of disbelief
wears off, and then the nonnegotiable reality of the loss starts to
set in. This is a truly painful and difficult time for most people.
There are tears, whether shed openly or not. Most will experience sleepless nights, extreme fatigue, and a loss of the ability to
concentrate. Some individuals experience other physical symptoms such as chest tightness or gastrointestinal upset. Others
report an almost disabling sensation of disorganization, distract-
ibility, and/or forgetfulness. Tasks that were once automatically performed become overwhelming. Balancing a checkbook
or cooking a meal can seem akin to an Olympic competitive
event. Those who had previously loved to read can't get through
a sentence, despite their intense desire to lose themselves in a
good book. At a time when the newly bereaved are seeking
internal reassurance that they can survive and make it on their
own, many are instead shaken to the core by a pervasive sense
of loss of control and basic inability to cope.

During this time of acute grieving, many individuals describe their grief as washing over them in powerful waves of
emotional pain and yearning. One moment you're almost fine
and the next moment you're a puddle on the floor. Many bereaved parents and newly widowed spouses poignantly report a
painful physical sensation in their heart or arms as they ache to
hold the lost one just one more time.

Some newly bereaved start to avoid social contact at this point, in an effort to eliminate the potential embarrassment of losing control in front of others. Social withdrawal can occur during acute grief for other reasons as well. Many otherwise charitable and kindly people find themselves disconcertingly jealous and resentful of intact families or happy-looking couples. It is also hard to find the energy to smile and participate in even the simplest of social interactions when one is so very sad, overwhelmed, and exhausted. It is also easier to avoid all of those unpredictable, but highly upsetting, social encounters when an uninformed acquaintance will innocently ask how your recently deceased loved one is doing. Despite all of these social hazards, acute grief is a time when comfort and companionship are often badly needed, although not to the exclusion of rest and quiet solitude.

Very, very gradually, the frequency and intensity of the acute pains of mourning start to lessen. This healing process will usually begin insidiously and gradually become more evident both to the bereaved and to others over time. Years ago, it was thought that most of us could totally resolve our grief in about six to nine months. That oversimplification is no longer thought to be true. After all, grief is hard work and it requires time. Grief is not something you can rush through, nor should you.

True adjustment to a significant loss and all of its related secondary losses will probably take several years, but before that occurs, the intense despair of acute grief will start to ever so slowly subside. There will be fewer bad days and a growing number of manageable or even good days. There will be more energy for everyday activities and a slowly renewing capacity to enjoy activities and time spent with friends. You will find yourself effortlessly smiling at a friend or laughing at a joke. Initially it feels strange, but you will get used to it again. Life has started to move on. It is a different life from the one before, but it is still your life, and worth making the best of.

THREE WIDOWS

Cheryl unexpectedly became a widow when she was just forty years old. Her children were ages six, four, and two when they lost their dad. Kevin, Cheryl's husband, was only forty-six when he suddenly dropped dead. Cheryl, a homemaker and mother, and Kevin, a fifth-grade teacher and track coach, had been competitive runners. They were both good-looking, slender, and physically fit. Neither had ever been seriously ill. They had been married for only eight years. Unfortunately, Kevin also had a rare but undiagnosed congenital heart defect that had insidiously enlarged and damaged his heart. In November 2006, Cheryl spoke to her husband briefly as he left for a state cross-country meet. Hours later, the unimaginable phone call came. Kevin had safely arrived at the race site, only to suddenly collapse and die of a massive heart attack.

Cheryl entered my office shortly after the first anniversary of Kevin's death. During her first year of widowhood, Cheryl had eagerly sought out various support services for her children and for herself. Sadly, Cheryl's father had died of a prolonged cancer only three short months after Kevin's death, so she was coping with the loss of two important men in her life.

Cheryl was trying valiantly to hold everything together, but a year later, it still felt like it was all falling apart. Cheryl was exhausted; she couldn't eat and couldn't stop crying. She couldn't stop thinking about the unfairness and unexpectedness of her young husband's death. She worried that Kevin had suffered in some way shortly before he died. She missed her dad, although she was more able to accept that his suffering was over. She worried that she would never feel whole again. Cheryl had been taking good care of her children, but she needed to take better care of herself.

Jamie, an accountant, was widowed at age sixty. Her husband, John, a retired salesman, was sixty-seven when he unexpectedly died. Jamie and John had been married thirty years. He had a prior marriage that had ended in divorce. They had no children together, but John had two grown daughters from his prior marriage. John was a stocky but strong man. He had suffered from some minor arthritic aches and pains first thing in the morning, but otherwise considered himself quite healthy. Jamie is a thin, attractive, and meticulously groomed middle-aged woman. She had been diagnosed with a gastrointestinal disorder about ten years prior to John's death and had been quite ill for some time, but her illness had been in remission for several years. In the spring of 2006, John and Jamie were all packed and ready for a long-awaited trip to visit his children and grandchildren out west. Tragically, Jamie woke up that morning but couldn't awaken her husband. John had suffered a fatal heart attack sometime during the night. He had died while she was asleep.

Jamie's primary-care physician referred her to my office five months after John's death. Jamie's physician was concerned that the stress of coping with John's tragic death had significantly decreased Jamie's physical stamina and was potentially increasing the likelihood of a flare-up of her preexisting medical ailment. Jamie had also experienced an episode of depression several years prior, so her doctor was concerned about a possible resurgence of that. For some, depression is a recurrent illness, and Jamie was clearly at risk for a second episode of clinical depression.

When Jamie first entered my office, she was frighteningly

thin, pale, and exhausted-looking. She was, however, calm and dry-eyed. She couldn't sleep. She couldn't eat without feeling sick to her stomach. She dragged herself to work every day, but struggled to concentrate and feared making a mistake. Jamie had never loved her job, but now it was a daily ordeal. Friends were trying to reach out and support her, but she was too tired to return their phone calls.

Ann was fifty-two when she was widowed. Her engineer husband, Matt, was fifty-four when he lost his eighteen-month battle to lung cancer. Their two sons were grown and out of the house. Matt was a tall, thin, soft-spoken man, who had suffered the trials and tribulations of his prolonged illness quietly and with great patience. Ann was a short, vivacious kindergarten teacher. At a distance, they looked odd together, but up close you could see how well they complemented each other. Ann had survived breast cancer eight years prior, but Matt had always been the healthy one. Matt was diagnosed in the fall of 2001. He spent much of that next year in and out of the hospital. But whenever he was well enough, he would return to work and spend as much time as possible with Ann and their two sons. Despite his progressing illness, they took some memorable family vacations and found time to laugh, enjoy, and reminisce. In March 2003, Matt died at home with hospice care support, surrounded by his grief-stricken wife and two sons.

Ann referred herself to my office last year. Matt had been dead for five years. Ann thought that she had adapted to widowhood and her new life reasonably well. It hadn't been easy, but she had done it. Ann hadn't sought out therapy per se; she had briefly attended a local widows' support group, which she found helpful because it was nice to know that she wasn't "the only one going through this."

But the month before she called my office, Ann had attended

the funeral of her husband's younger sister, who had died unexpectedly in a car accident. Ann was disturbed by the intensity of her reaction to this second family funeral. Everything was too familiar; it brought back too many memories. Ann began to wonder if perhaps she hadn't adapted as well as she had previously thought.

Ann had always been a feisty and independent woman. She was charmingly outspoken and entered my office looking comfortable but tired and concerned. She hadn't slept well since her sister-in-law's funeral service. The memories of Matt's illness and death, which had quieted fairly significantly in the last several years, were again more vivid. "I thought that I was done with this part," she commented with more than a little frustration.

COMMON QUESTIONS

When is grief no longer "normal"? When has someone grieved too long? What is the difference between grief and depression? If grief is a normal part of life, why see a therapist or go to a support group?

When we lose someone we love, we experience many losses, not just one. We grieve the actual physical losses; we grieve the symbolic losses. We grieve what we have lost in the present and what we thought we would have in the future.

For example, when Cheryl unexpectedly lost Kevin, she lost not only her husband, but the father of her children, a co-parent, a running partner, and her best friend. She lost her vision of the future, along with her status as a married woman amongst her married and coupled friends. For some, widowhood also means a drastically changed financial status, raising issues of employment changes or downsizing one's housing situation. So of course, grieving takes time.

SOME ANSWERS

Cheryl's, Jamie's, and Ann's stories help us to answer some of the questions alluded to earlier. Grief is worthy of treatment if it threatens your physical well-being, which is what Jamie's physician was concerned about. Treatment may also be indicated if you have tried everything that you can and just feel that the suffering is too intense. This was Cheryl's dilemma. Grief and clinical depression are not the same entities, but they share some similar characteristics and may coexist, especially when the bereaved has had a prior personal history or a strong family history of depression. Grief heals with time; clinical depression usually requires treatment. In Jamie's case, her symptoms were consistent enough with depression that her doctor decided to start her on antidepressant medication in addition to her work with me.

Lastly, the grieving for and missing of a loved one can last a lifetime, but usually the acute distress dissipates over time. But so-called anniversary reactions are not uncommon, whether occurring over holidays, birthdays, the anniversary of the death, or the second family funeral that Ann experienced. Fortunately these anniversary reactions tend to be time-limited, and not as intense as the initial phase of acute grief.

THREE TASKS

The goals of the grieving that we do, either in or outside of a therapy office, include our need to accept the loss, survive the pain of that loss, and find a meaningful way to adjust to a world and a life without the person we have loved and lost. These three tasks sound so simple, but anyone who has gone through this process knows how very difficult and complex the work of grief really is. Most of my clients indicate that narrative disclosure— the act of putting upsetting experiences into words, whether written or oral—facilitates this healing process. This technique certainly occurs in a therapist's office, but it also can take place with a trusted confidante or in the privacy of your home when journaling with a pen or on your computer.

Signs of healthy grief resolution include the bereaved individuals feeling that life still has meaning and purpose. Despite the pain and disruption of their loss, they still trust themselves and the world around them. Daily life has structure, a reasonable amount of activity, and they have remained or returned to being open to positive social relationships. The goals of successful mourning are not to stop missing our loved one or to replace that person. The goals of healthy grief resolution are not to forget but to remember and appreciate what was, while still being able to be hopeful about whatever is ahead.

When you are acutely grieving, grief lasts an unbearably long time, but fortunately for most of us, it does not have to last forever. Grief is a process with a beginning, middle, and eventually a healing resolution. To grieve also means we have loved.

What we have once enjoyed and deeply loved we can never lose, for all that we love deeply becomes a part of us.

—HELEN KELLER

Therefore, grief is an accommodation or an adjustment; it is not about forgetting or even recovering. Grief changes us. It hurts us. It makes us sadder, but it can also make us stronger and wiser. Grief can soften and humble us; it reminds us that life and loved ones are not to be taken for granted. Life, love, and meaningful relationships are precious gifts that come with few guarantees. Fateful events in our lives can unfold over years or in mere seconds. Grief can lead us to more acutely appreciate what we had, what we still have, and even what we will have someday.

A client of mine likened acute grief to an unwelcome relative who had come to their home, uninvited but for a prolonged visit. For a while, this intrusive houseguest disrupted everything and demanded constant attention. But eventually, the unwanted guest adjusted to the family's routine and the visit became less distasteful. And then the guest moved next door, visiting only occasionally. Acute grief is very much like this unpleasant intruder. For a while it takes over your home and your life. But at some point in time, grief will need to move on and so then will we. I believe that this analogy is both a common and useful one.

ENDINGS AND BEGINNINGS

Cheryl is running again. She looks healthy and well. Her three young children have adjusted to their new single-parent family life. They are doing well in school and are busy with friends and extracurricular activities. Cheryl doesn't feel ready to date yet, but she can think about it now without getting upset or feeling guilty. She still misses Kevin but is also very grateful for the incredibly special time that they had together.

Jamie is sleeping again. She has regained much of the lost weight and once again has the energy for friends and social activities. So far, her health is stable. Therapy allowed Jamie to express the feelings she had been internalizing. Antidepressant medication helped her to sleep, regain her strength, and find the energy to reconnect with friends. Once feeling better, Jamie made the decision to leave her old accounting position. She now runs a catering business with a close girlfriend. They're not making very much money yet, but she loves every minute of it.

Ann has again moved on. Once she understood her unexpected anniversary reaction, she was less frightened by it. Ann is thinking about retirement, but still loves teaching. She is dating a nice man. "He is very different from Matt, but he is a good man, and I'm lucky to have him in my life." Ann recently started volunteering at a local church, and she is running a support group for recent widows.

LESSONS LEARNED

Cheryl and I recently had our last therapy session. She feels ready to "graduate" and move on. I asked her what she had learned from her grief experience and her thoughts about grief therapy. Cheryl's answers are gifts to anyone who has experienced the loss of a loved one and is seeking comfort.

"I have learned that I can survive the unimaginable. And I have learned that time heals." Cheryl added, "Therapy saved my life and my sanity. It reined me in. It helped me to understand what I was going through and why. It gave me hope; hope that this pain didn't have to be forever and hope that there was a light at the end of the tunnel, even if I couldn't see or feel it."

Weeping may linger for the night, but joy comes with the morning.

—PSALM 30

Chapter Eight

FAMILIES

Home is the place where, when you have to go there,
They have to take you in.

—ROBERT FROST

FAMILY CONTEXT

The family plays a major role in the world of health and illness. Most family units are the source of their individual members' health beliefs and practices. The biologic family system is the source of our shared genetic risk, or lack thereof, for certain illnesses. Family stress may contribute to any of a number of so-called stress-related illnesses. But family support can be an invaluable contributor to an individual's recovery from a major medical illness or after surgery.

Serious illness also affects an entire family, not just the ill family member. It may be the individual who is sick, but usually the entire family is hurting. Similarly, individuals grieve, but this often occurs within the context of a family unit. After the loss of a loved one, a complex juggling act occurs as various relatives attempt to process their own loss and support others at the same time.

Families and family life have changed over the years. For

example, we have more single-parent families and dual-career families, but fewer families living in the same city than in prior generations. Yet families, whether near or distant, still play a powerful and pivotal role in many of our lives. A family can be a major source of support and comfort during difficult times; a family can also add stress and conflict to an already challenging situation. Some families do a little bit of both.

Family therapists teach us that a family is more than a mere collection of individual members. It is a group of people who are connected in many ways, including biologically, emotionally, and/or financially. It is also a group of people with a shared history and an intended future. Therefore the ties that bind these individual family members together are complex. Even families that share similar neighborhood locations and socio-economic characteristics along with identical cultural backgrounds may look alike on the outside but will still be very different on the inside. Each family grouping is unique.

The family unit also has work to do, just like the rest of us. It is the family's job to physically protect its young members and to socialize them so that they can live successfully in the world outside the family walls. Our families are also supposed to promote in each of us a sense of belonging and connectedness along with a sense of competence and positive self-worth. Family groups, just like individuals, also have to cope with various expected and unexpected changes over time, solve problems, and mediate differences among individual members. It isn't easy being a functional family. Family theorists suggest that in order for a family unit to be functionally healthy, good problem-solving skills, good decision-making skills, good communication skills, and adequate resources are required.

Families also grow up over time, just as individuals do. So there are newly formed families and families with very young,

school-age, or adolescent children, as well as empty-nest families and those with adult children or even grandchildren. Each
family unit has its own leadership style: For example, some
families are leaderless, others are patriarchal, matriarchal, or
very egalitarian. Can you remember who made the decisions
in the family that you grew up in? Was it always the same person? Within our families, most people have explicit and implicit roles. For example, there is the person who takes out the
garbage, disciplines the children, or pays the bills. If there are
children, there will be the oldest and the baby. Less obviously,
many families may have a peacemaker, a troublemaker, a star,
or a black sheep.

Each family unit also has its own style; some are very close
and protective, while others are more distant. Some family
systems are highly emotive, while others are quite reserved.
All families face the daunting task of trying to figure out how
to balance the needs of their individual members with the
well-being of the larger family unit. So daily family life can be
pretty interesting and quite complex. Serious illness and grief
only serve to add to the challenges that our families are already
coping with.

A life-threatening illness or a recent death can be a potential
family crisis. The determinants of how any particular family
group will respond to these types of crises include the family's
available supports, its resources, and its prior experiences with
similar stresses; other concurrent stresses or issues; the nature
of the relationships among all the individual members and between each member and the ill or recently lost loved one; each
member's perceptions or expectations about what should or
will be happening next; and dynamics such as role flexibility
or capacity for coming to a consensus. This is a long list of

complex variables that come together and factor into each and every family's unique response to illness or grief. Each family unit has its own unique strengths and weaknesses. My belief is that most families, like most individuals, are truly trying to do the best they can to cope with the multiple challenges inherent in each serious illness or loss experience.

The notion of role flexibility is important because the family that is able to more comfortably take on one another's family jobs or accept outside help may be at a significant advantage during such crises. How a serious illness or recent death will affect a family also depends upon the specific impact of that illness or loss. For example, was the ill or deceased member the major financial provider of the household, the primary decision maker, or a significant source of emotional support?

Like individuals during times of extreme stress, families in crisis can respond in either helpful or unhelpful ways. Some families will pull together, some families will pull apart, and some families will do one and then the other. All families coping with serious illness or grief are likely to experience some degree of increased emotional and physical strain, as well as stress due to differing expectations regarding the juggling of responsibilities or the division of family assets after a death.

Additionally, each family will understandably need to negotiate the increased uncertainty wrought by a life-threatening illness or death of a close family member. Other possible hurdles might include financial strain, possible social isolation due to either the demands of illness or a new grief, and any spiritual angst brought to bear as each family member finds their own way to make peace with a loved one's illness, suffering, and/or death.

THE JUGGLING ACT: ILLNESS AND THE FAMILY

When someone in a family is facing a life-threatening illness, everyone else in that family must find a way to simultaneously support their dying loved one but also to deal with their own fears and needs. In Randy Pausch's book *The Last Lecture*, he alluded to this phenomenon when discussing one of our early therapy sessions. It was August, and Randy had recently been told that he might have only three to six months longer to live. He had also been asked to give Carnegie Mellon University's "Last Lecture" that fall. "Last Lecture" series are common on many academic campuses, and it is considered quite an honor to be asked to participate. Randy wanted to give the lecture. His wife, Jai, disagreed. They came to my office to resolve this very real and troubling disagreement.

Jai and Randy were clearly committed to each other and to their three young children. They had approached the many challenges of Randy's recently diagnosed pancreatic cancer as a marital team. But that shared reality didn't change the fact that they still held two different positions and thus two different perspectives in their family's cancer journey. Randy was the person doing the dying, and Jai was the future widow.

Jai, understandably, wanted Randy's precious remaining time to be spent with their children and with her. Jai and Randy had only been married seven years and their children were quite young. Jai was struggling to grasp the new reality that cancer had delivered to their doorstep. She and Randy would not be spending the next twenty years raising their children together. From Jai's perspective, the time Randy would need to prepare for, travel to, and deliver this lecture was time their family couldn't afford to give away. After all, their children would soon be without a father. Randy would be leaving her permanently, soon enough.

But Randy was a young and previously healthy, active, and professionally competitive man who was struggling to get used to the idea that both his life and his promising academic career were about to be cut short. This last opportunity to show his worth as a teacher, to say good-bye to valued colleagues, and perhaps to leave a lasting legacy for both his students and his children, was hard to let go of. Randy was not quite ready to surrender to his illness; he was not ready to go home and wait to die. He had something more to say.

Jai and Randy were both right, when viewed from their personal perspectives. But a decision still had to be made. The therapeutic solution was deceptively simple. I asked Randy and Jai to talk to each other, not to me, and to explain their respective positions as best they could. They then would need to decide on how to best meet both of their needs to the extent that was possible. Randy and Jai spoke quietly to each other, holding hands and looking into each other's eyes. They took turns and when not speaking, they listened. They truly listened.

> *Disagreements cannot be resolved and the needed compromises cannot be made until we learn how to listen to each other.*

As many readers already know, Randy gave his last lecture. Jai was in the audience that day, so they shared the moment as a couple. Randy's lecture has been transformed into a living legacy of hope and inspiration for a worldwide audience. More important, Randy found a way to leave behind a message for his children about the values and the hopes that he so wished he could have provided in person, when they were old enough to understand. Jai and Randy found their right answer, and they found it together.

Randy and Jai worked hard on their marriage until the day Randy died. They were committed to traveling this sad family journey the best way possible. Randy juggled his own emotional and physical suffering with his commitment to the heart-wrenching task of preparing his wife and young children for family life without him. Jai balanced her own anticipatory grief and fear of approaching widowhood with her demanding day-to-day roles as a mother to three young children and caregiver to her dying husband.

THE JUGGLING ACT: GRIEF AND THE FAMILY

This emotional misalignment between loving and supportive family members or spouses is common during serious illnesses such as Randy's cancer and during a family's experience with grief. Although everyone in a family may have experienced the same loss, they will each perceive and express it differently. After all, grief may be a family crisis, but it is also an individual journey. Each grieving family member will attempt to come to grips with personal loss in his or her own unique fashion. However, these individual pathways through grief are occurring at a time when family unity is usually called for and even expected.

Joan and Sam came to my office for a consultation six months after losing their son, Donny, to a hit-and-run car accident. Donny, their only child, was eighteen and a high school senior at the time when his young life ended. This exhausted, bereaved couple sought counseling not because they expected any relief from the still-new grieving process, but because they were concerned that their marriage was failing.

Joan and Sam had married in their early twenties, and until recently had rarely ever argued or spent time apart. Their marriage had been the envy of all of their friends. They had expected to grieve in tandem, crying together and supporting each other through each difficult new day. But instead, they seemed to be drifting apart. Each was angry and hurt by the other's lack of support and disappointed in the apparently flawed marital bond.

Since Donny's death, Joan had taken a leave from her part-time sales position at a local department store. She cried daily and struggled to get through each long day. Sam, an engineer, had done the opposite: He was working longer hours than ever before and never seemed to express any visible sadness or grief. Sam tried to cheer Joan up, but she resented him for it. Joan tried to get Sam to talk more about Donny's death, but he resisted. They were stuck.

As with Randy and Jai, I asked Joan and Sam to take turns describing to each other what their grief for Donny had been like so far. Joan described her considerable pain, but also shared that crying and talking about Donny was actually helpful to her. These emotive mechanisms were her way through the grief.

Sam shared that he was struggling to be strong for his grief-stricken wife. He avoided crying or getting upset in front of Joan because, "If I break down and cry in front of you, we'll both drown." Meanwhile, Sam cried alone every morning in the shower, where Joan couldn't hear him. Sam's long hours at work were healing to him: It gave him a sense of purpose when he otherwise felt lost.

Joan and Sam were both grieving; they were just going about it differently. Once they better understood these different responses to a shared grief, they once again felt more united and better positioned to support each other. Sam now understood that talking to Joan about Donny wouldn't add to her suffering, but it might make her feel less alone. Joan understood that Sam's work hours were not intended as an abandonment of her, just a different means of getting through the grief.

The best way out is always through.

—ROBERT FROST

SOMETIMES CHILDREN KNOW BEST

A colleague of mine recently celebrated her fifty-fifth birthday. It was a bittersweet celebration. Within this last year, my friend learned that her breast cancer of many years ago had returned and metastasized to her liver. The last several months of treatment have considerably slowed the spread of her disease, and on most days this very special woman puts a smile on her face as she copes with the time bomb living in her abdomen. But birthdays are special, because they bring together our past, present, and hoped-for future.

My friend did not want to "play the cancer card," but she had quietly hoped that her husband, two grown children, and other close relatives or friends would recognize the powerful symbolism of this year's birthday celebration, when the likelihood of others was so very uncertain. Having a serious illness is essentially an isolating experience. And when you do it as gracefully as this strong woman did, it was easy for those around her to lose sight of how much of a struggle it really was.

This year's milestone birthday fell on a weekday. Out-of-town relatives and family friends delivered the requisite birthday wishes over the phone, but they were cheery and brief, with no mention of the powerful contexts of cancer treatment or survival. As my friend said, "It was as if it was just another birthday." Admittedly, these individuals had the best of intentions, and probably just didn't want to bring up anything potentially upsetting on an otherwise happy occasion. But by ignoring the powerful reality of cancer survivorship that my friend battled every day, they had inadvertently contributed to her feelings of aloneness and lack of appreciation for what she was going through.

Unfortunately this pattern of unintentional hurtfulness continued. Her son and his wife called and asked if the evening's birthday dinner could be postponed until the upcoming weekend in order to ease their dual career workday pressures. My colleague's loving but forgetful husband admitted that he had forgotten to get her either a card or a gift, although clearly he would be happy to get her whatever she wanted: She just had to tell him what to get. My now hurting friend told her husband not to worry and agreed to postpone the evening's birthday dinner in order to ease any inconvenience. She felt very alone and unloved, not because she didn't know that all of these people loved her, but because it felt as if they didn't understand what she was going through.

My friend's daughter, Annie, was the last to call. When informed about the rescheduling of the upcoming dinner celebration, she asked if she could quickly stop by anyway since she would be doing errands nearby. Her tired, somewhat depressed mother reluctantly agreed to a short visit. Annie entered her mother's house without knocking, and as her mother turned to greet her youngest child, my friend noticed the incredibly short tousled haircut that her beautiful auburn-haired daughter was wearing. Annie had had long tresses down her back, but now her hair was almost as short as the growth that her post-cancer-treatment mother sported under her wig. Annie shyly smiled and announced, "They needed at least ten inches in order to make a wig for cancer patients, but I gave them fourteen."

In that moment, Annie healed her mother's heart. Her birthday gift to her mother was the gift of understanding. This generous, symbolic gesture said everything my friend needed to hear. She was told in a language more powerful than words that she was loved; that her pain and struggle were neither forgotten, minimized, nor underappreciated; and that her continued existence was celebrated and not taken for granted. All of my friend's family members love her, but Annie had found the grace and courage to acknowledge the painfully frightening reality in their midst, and by doing so, had made her mother feel less alone.

COMMUNICATION IS THE KEY

The family challenges of serious illness or grief are complex and intricate. Emotional discrepancies like those experienced by Jai and Randy, or Joan and Sam, are more common than not. Despite the respective strengths of these two couples, being the one who is sick is a different journey from being the spouse who bears witness, and similarly, even among very cohesive marital partners, we each grieve differently.

It is hard to support an ill or grieving loved one when you yourself are hurting. It is irksome to consider compromises when you are already very stressed, overwhelmed, and also convinced that you are right this time. And yet in the midst of a crisis, family members may need to make multiple compromises in the name of family unity. It is hard to be angry with someone who is very sick, but also hard not to be. After all, who is leaving whom in that situation?

It is difficult to be flexible and take on more roles and responsibilities when a family member becomes ill or dies. Many new widows can attest to the challenges involved in learning to do home repairs while grieving acutely. It is never easy to attend to the needs of individuals within a family and the family group at the same time, but that task becomes much more cumbersome when it takes place during a family crisis.

Family members understandably struggle to agree about decisions ranging from nursing-home placement for an ailing elderly parent to how best to celebrate the first holiday season after Mom's death. Again, these disagreements usually represent heartfelt discrepancies between individual perceptions regarding what the correct solution really is. Family squabbles over a deceased member's assets or material belongings may reflect preexisting schisms and a longstanding history of unresolved conflicts, or they may be a more transitory manifestation over the need to have been loved more or most by the recently lost relative.

A neighbor of mine recently stopped over for a cup of coffee. Carol was clearly distraught, and she readily shared that she and her sister had recently argued about their late mother's will. The item in contention was a ruby ring. Carol was the elder of the two sisters, and her mother had left the ruby ring to her oldest child in her will. But Carol's younger sister had lived closer to their mother and had been their mother's caretaker during the last two years of this woman's life. So baby sister Ellen had indicated that she thought the valuable ring should belong to her instead of the favored eldest. After all, she had earned it.

Carol wanted the ring but also acknowledged the great burden her younger sister had accepted during the last two years of taking care of their ailing parent. I asked my neighbor, "What means more to you—the ring, or your relationship with Ellen?"

My neighbor frowned and then smiled. "Thanks, that was easier than I thought it would be."

Later, Carol shared that she had called Ellen and quickly stated, "I don't want us to argue anymore about Mom's ring. I like the ring very much, but I love you. If having that ring will make you feel closer to our mother and feel more appreciated for all of your sacrifices when she was ill, well then, it's yours with all my love." Once the emotional impasse was resolved, the two sisters were able to move forward. Ellen did keep the ruby ring, but she gave her older sister a portrait in her possession that had been in their family for many years. Both sisters were happy with their respective treasures. More important, they were once again a united family.

Communication is key to resolving each of these dilemmas. Disagreements are a normal and inevitable part of family life. The heightened emotional strain and differing emotional experiences that occur during a family crisis of serious illness or recent death only serve to contribute to the likelihood of miscommunication or conflict.

And yet many, if not all, family members do resolve these potential stumbling blocks and manage to support one another as well. Most families do rally and come together during times of illness and grief. And if your family has or does, it is something to be proud of. The sad exception to this optimistic prediction usually involves family situations whereby a recent crisis is unfortunately superimposed over years and years of unresolved and bitter conflict. The latter situation usually requires a more intensive, therapeutic intervention such as ongoing family therapy.

However, for most families several basic communication guidelines will suffice. Realistic expectations should be the basis for any difficult decisions made during an illness- or grief-related family crisis. So family members should do their homework whether the dilemma is nursing-home placement, funeral arrangements, or grief resolution. Illness and grief create a plethora of feelings, expectations, hopes, and fears, but some are more realistic than others. Consultation with a physician, lawyer, financial advisor, or grief counselor may be a necessary step toward gathering the needed information to make sure everyone in the family is on the same proverbial page.

The goals of family discussions during these exhausting and painful times should initially be listening and understanding, versus immediate agreement and consensus. Feeling heard and understood during a time of hurt or stress is innately healing. Once someone feels listened to and understood, they are more likely to be open to hearing another's feelings and perceptions. Paradoxically, good communication is more about listening than talking.

Once family members have made a genuine effort to listen to and understand other family members, then it is time to seek solutions to whatever the group dilemma might be. Consensus might not always be possible, but compromises usually are. Randy and Jai were able to find a satisfactory compromise because they cared enough about each other to listen despite strong differences in opinion. Joan and Sam breached the chasm of their differing approaches to grief simply by better understanding the other's bereavement experience. Carol and Ellen were able to remember that they were sisters as well as daughters, and that family treasures are a poor substitute for a live sibling. These resolutions are not about winners and losers: They are about caring, listening, and understanding.

Understanding what your loved ones or relatives are going through, and how it affects their perceptions and behaviors, is the all-important step toward supporting them and helping them to find a way to support you.

Chapter Nine

GRIEVING CHILDREN

A child can ask questions that a wise man cannot answer.

—AUTHOR UNKNOWN

A CHILD'S GRIEF

Bereavement is not an adults-only experience. For many young children, their first introduction to death will be via the loss of a pet. However, each year a significant number of young children will also experience the loss of a parent, sibling, other relative, or a close friend. Since we may not be able to protect all of our children from the upset of a serious illness or loss of a loved one, we should do our best to teach them about these inevitable life experiences so that they will be better able to understand and cope with these challenges, whether they arise during childhood or later in life.

Interestingly, there are some parallels between childhood grief and adult grief. The basic tasks of bereavement are the same, regardless of age. Young and old will need to understand and come to terms with the reality of the loss, grieve the loss in their own fashion, and then find a way to remember but go on. Similarly, childhood grief, like adult grief, often involves multiple losses and changes. For example, after the loss of a parent, a child's family may need to move. This relocation will then result in changes in school and peer groups for the recently bereaved child. The remaining parent may need to return to work, work longer hours, and/or simply be less emotionally available while struggling with his or her own acute grief. Every single one of these changes in the previous status quo looms quite large in the life of a child.

TRYING TO BE GOOD

Ricky was an adorable, blond-haired and blue-eyed little boy who had just turned four. He had an impish and loving personality and generally made all of the adults around him smile. Until recently, Ricky had also been a reasonably well-behaved little boy. But now he was "acting out" and causing his parents undue additional stress. Their family had just lost Ricky's sister, three-month-old Rachel, to Sudden Infant Death Syndrome (SIDS). Mom and Dad had done their best to explain this unexpected loss to young Ricky, but of course they were having trouble understanding it themselves.

Just when these newly grieving parents needed Ricky to behave, he was digging up his own and the neighbor's backyards. The neighbor was a kind older woman and had been understanding at first, but now enough was enough. A play session in my office helped us to understand Ricky's seemingly illogical and disruptive behavior.

Taking his lead from his favorite bedtime story, "Jack and the Beanstalk," Ricky had been secretly taking green beans from the family's refrigerator and "planting" them in his and his neighbor's backyards. He was hoping to grow a beanstalk, so that he could go visit his baby sister and bring her some toys and a blanket just in case she was cold. Little Ricky was just trying to be a good big brother to his baby sister.

Four-and-a-half-year-old Cindy's grief took the opposite tack. Following the unexpected death of her father, a young soldier, she was so amazingly well behaved that it made her wise mother nervous. Cindy never cried and she never sulked. For weeks she went to bed without protest and played quietly, demanding little attention. Usually a fussy eater, Cindy ate everything placed on her plate without complaint. During a therapeutic storytelling session in my office, Cindy was able to haltingly explain that she was trying "really hard to be good, so that Daddy would stop being mad at me and come back home." Poor Cindy had nearly exhausted herself trying so hard to be "Daddy's good little girl."

LITTLE TEARS

Young children are not simply little adults. They behave differently from us, and they think differently also. After all, these youngsters are learning language as they grow and figuring out the world around them along the way. Even though young children may speak the same language that we do, they may mean something quite different from even their parents' initial interpretation.

This brings to mind the old joke about a father who is at home supervising his five-year-old son's play activities while his wife is out shopping. His son and two neighborhood friends are playing reasonably quietly in the backyard, and Dad is inside contentedly watching television. Their home was nestled into a two-year-old housing development. Hence all of the neighbors were relative newcomers, but his son had made fast friends with several similar-aged peers. All of a sudden, the man's son bursts into the room saying, "Dad, I need to know where I came from—you know, how did I get here?" The somewhat flustered father automatically responds, "Why don't you wait until your mother gets home and she'll tell you all about it." "But Dad, I need to know *now*: All the other boys know." So the poorly prepared and now embarrassed parent starts to ramble through an abbreviated version of the "birds and the bees." Once again his young son impatiently interrupts, "No, Dad, not that stuff, I meant like Chicago or New York. You know, where did I come from and how did we wind up here?"

Since children behave, think, and even communicate somewhat differently from their adult counterparts, understandably they also grieve somewhat differently. Any child's grief response will be determined by his or her individual personality style and behavioral temperament. So like adult grief, each grief reaction will be unique to that child in some ways. Young children tend to have shorter attention spans than most adults, so they can often seem to grieve one moment and nonchalantly go off to play the next. This on-again, off-again response to loss can be disconcerting to the surrounding adults, but it is usually simply a developmental manifestation of attentional immaturity. A child's grief, in large part, will be determined by how they understand the concept of death. And generally, a child's understanding of death is age-dependent.

AGES AND STAGES

Infants and toddlers (birth to two years old) are too young to understand death per se, but they may react to the upset and distress of others around them. Children this young explore the world through movement and senses such as touch, taste, and smell, not thoughts. They are also very reactive to any changes in their usual daily routine. So these little ones are at risk for becoming irritable or sleep-deprived during stressful family times.

Preschoolers (ages two to six) are imaginative little people and they tend to view death as something reversible or temporary, like "making believe" during playtime. Preschoolers are the young children most likely to ask when their deceased loved one will come back, despite repeated explanations that reappearance is not possible. It is hard to understand "forever" when you can't quite grasp tomorrow, next week, or next year. Gradually, however, gentle, consistent reminders that the lost loved one is dead and cannot come back, but that it is OK to miss that person very much, will help these children absorb the confusing cognitive concept of permanence.

Developmental theorists declare this era the time of "magical thinking." This is the all-too-brief time when anything we can imagine is possible: Dolls and stuffed animals come to life, and if you tie a red towel around a youngster's neck, he becomes Superman. These young ones are also quite sensitive to the emotions of those around them. Steven and Cindy are both examples of this developmental version of childhood grief.

Young school-age children (ages six to nine) are beginning to grasp the permanence and universality (it will happen to everyone at some point in time) of death. But these youngsters are still easily confused and at risk for blaming themselves for a loved one's death because they have misbehaved in some way. This is the time when young children are leaving the home for the first time and beginning to regularly interact with teachers and peers. They are competing for the first time. They are being tested and graded for the first time. So it's easy to see why they might think "When anything bad happens, it must be my fault." These young school-age children may also perceive death as possibly contagious. In other words, they may start to worry that since one person in the family has died, maybe others in the family might also die.

Older school-age children (ages nine to twelve) are continuing to develop the understanding of death as something irreversible, universal, and inevitable, but they are still confused by the details of how it all works. They are still young enough to view death as punishment for wrongdoing. School age represents the developmental quiet before the storm of adolescent angst and rebellion. These children tend to be fairly concrete, and they live in a world with rules: Games have rules, teachers have rules, and school has rules. These rule-bound children tend to ask a lot of fairly specific questions that may seem morbid to adults but are really just their age-appropriate mechanism for sorting it all out.

ALL CHILDREN

These developmental stages are meant to be general guidelines to help us to better understand what a child might be thinking and feeling about the loss of a loved one. But any child's reactions will be uniquely his or her own. All children, however, need to know that a loved one's death was not their fault. They need to know that there are still adults who will love and care for them, no matter who in the family has died.

Most children will benefit from the opportunity to return to their normal routines and activities. Younger children will need to be gently reminded that the dead loved one cannot come back, but that it is all right to miss that person very much. Grieving children need to know it is OK to be sad, and OK to ask questions. It is not possible to protect the child of a bereaved family from grief, but it is desirable to support them as they grieve, and to help them to understand this unfortunately early introduction into a very adult-like world. So being exposed to grieving adults within the family is not necessarily a bad thing.

Other useful guidelines for adults attempting to support a grieving child include: Know your own beliefs regarding death and afterlife, begin any conversation by finding out what the child is thinking or feeling, be present through touch and dedicated "special time," allow and encourage feelings, avoid praising stoicism, encourage remembrance, and encourage questions. It is also best to share the sad news gently and simply, but truthfully. It is wise to avoid fanciful or fairy tale–like explanations, even though they might be intended to soften the harsher reality. Children don't need a lot of detail unless they ask questions requesting it, but they do need honesty from the adults they trust.

Additionally, protective factors that have been shown to facilitate a young child's grief resolution include: minimal changes, if at all possible, in the child's environment; a consistent adult figure or figures to attend sensitively to the child's daily needs; bereaved adults who encourage discussion, sharing sadness, and sharing memories openly; and the feeling of being accepted and understood by peers.

CHILDREN'S QUESTIONS

The questions that children ask about death, dying, and funerals are pretty amazing sometimes. They can make you stop and think. Actually, you probably should stop and think before you answer. In general, explanations should be kept simple, using age-appropriate language. Younger children tend to ask questions like: *"What is dead? What made them die? Where did they go? When will they be back? Who will take care of me? Why did they want to leave? Where is heaven and can I go visit? If you get sick, will you die too?"* Slightly older children tend to ask more concrete questions such as: *"What happens to the body after it's buried? What does a soul look like? Does it hurt when your heart stops? Do we feel anything after we're dead?"*

These questions make sense from a child's confused perspective but can be understandably painful for a newly grieving adult to answer. The answers to these and many other questions have to be based on the particular circumstances surrounding the death, as well as the cultural or spiritual context of the family involved in the loss. In general, the answers should also provide the reassurances mentioned previously and avoid using euphemisms for death such as sleeping or going on a long trip. After all, you don't want your little one to be afraid to fall asleep every night in fear that death will come visiting again. Neither do you want a child to become fearful every time someone in the family packs a suitcase. It is usually best to explain death in simple, physiological terms such as a time when the heart stops beating and the person stops breathing because the body is just too sick to work anymore, so everything stops. Similarly, the cause of death should be explained honestly but simply whether it be due to a specific illness, an accident, or some other circumstance. In most cases, children can be reassured that their lost loved one did not want to leave them. In fact, even in the case of a suicidal death, the loved one's actions and judgments were most likely distorted by a depressive illness and/or substance-use disorder, so again not reflective of a lack of love for those left behind. Answers to questions about heaven or the soul or specific burial practices are clearly specific to the cultural and spiritual beliefs of individual families and so cannot be answered generically. However, helpful hints regarding how to talk to children about death can be found among the recommended resources listed in the back of this book.

PARENTS' QUESTIONS

Parents of grieving children also have questions. *"Should my (three-year-old, eight-year-old, or eleven-year-old) go to the funeral?"*

Beth and Jimmy were siblings, ages six and four. Their parents gave them their first pet, a small turtle, for Christmas last year. They named the turtle Tommy. Unfortunately, Tommy the turtle lived a short life, and by April he had succumbed to whatever illnesses take turtles.

Beth and Jimmy noticed Tommy's absence right away and ran quickly to their father for an explanation of the turtle's seeming disappearance. The father gently told the two youngsters that their little pet had gotten sick and died. "But where is he?" they asked. The young father hesitated for a moment and then shared that since the death had occurred quite early in the morning, he had taken it upon himself to bury Tommy next door in the fenced-in field that abutted their property.

Beth and Jimmy seemed to comfortably accept this explanation and went off without further ado to have breakfast. However, after breakfast they of course gathered their respective pink and blue pails and shovels and went in search of Tommy the turtle. An hour later, two very tired, dirty, and sweaty children dispiritedly returned to the house having been unsuccessful in their search for their buried friend. The siblings' father then reluctantly admitted that he hadn't buried Tommy at all, but due to the early hour and Tommy's small size, he had simply flushed him down the toilet. Beth and Jimmy were horrified. "But we didn't get to say good-bye," they said almost simultaneously. The family then hurriedly decided to hold a brief memorial service in Tommy the turtle's honor. Clearly, even young children seem to sense the importance of rituals and saying good-bye.

Cultural practices vary considerably, but in general it is now thought that giving children the opportunity to take part in a formal mourning ritual, such as a funeral, can be helpful. There are several caveats. The child should be given an age-appropriate explanation of what will occur during the funeral and offered the choice of whether to attend. If a child chooses to go to the funeral, there should be a close relative or family friend (preferably someone familiar to the child) to keep the child company during the service. This caretaking arrangement allows young children to leave and play elsewhere when they become restless or bored. It allows slightly older children to be distracted from some of the emotional intensity involved in what is usually a really long day.

Children should be given other opportunities to memorialize their loved one, whether they attend a funeral or not. Drawing pictures to leave at the gravesite; helping to plant flowers at the gravesite or a memorial tree or shrub in the backyard; and making a memory scrapbook are all helpful activities to help children express their grief.

In this way, we are teaching our children as we are learning ourselves that grief doesn't mean forgetting; it means remembering as we live on.

"My wife has been diagnosed with lung cancer. She has started treatment, but the doctors are very concerned. What do we tell our young children?" This is a truly heartbreaking task, no matter what ages the involved children are. In this instance, the goal is to gradually educate and prepare the children of a seriously ill parent for whatever prognostic reality lies ahead.

When very young children are involved, it makes sense to wait until the ill parent starts to display signs of illness. Otherwise being told that Mommy is seriously ill when she looks and acts fine is awfully confusing. Older children, with their more sophisticated sense of time, may be told closer to the actual time of diagnosis. All children should be told some age-appropriate version of the fact that their mother has a serious illness called cancer and the doctors are working very hard to help her to get better. The children can then be reassured that their mother wants to get better very badly and that this illness is not anyone's fault.

This is usually enough information to start with. It will be more helpful at this point to prompt a child for any questions or worries than to add a lot of unnecessary details to an already overwhelming message. Either during this conversation or some time after, most children will ask some version of *"What if Mommy doesn't get better?"* or *"Is Mommy going to die?"* It is best to be honest: *"I don't know for sure, but I hope not. The doctors are doing everything that they can and so is Mommy. So for now, let's help Mommy to rest and hope that she starts to feel better soon. But if Mommy can't get better, remember that the rest of the family and I are all here to help take care of you. You will not be alone. Meanwhile, if you have any more questions, you can ask me whatever you want to know. And I promise to let you know what is going on, OK?"*

There is no way to totally protect children from the upset of a seriously ill or dying parent. But it is possible to gently prepare them for this harsh reality and to avoid leaving them uninformed and unsupported. An early grief experience will inevitably affect children, but it does not have to permanently damage them.

Children who are surrounded by much family love and consistency following the loss of a parent or other significant family member will heal, grow, and perhaps be strengthened by this experience in some way.

EXTRA HELP AS NEEDED

Like adults, grieving children deserve all of the help and support that they might need to get through this experience. Some young children benefit from several individual sessions with a therapist; others find support groups run specifically for children who have lost family members to be helpful. Certainly, any grieving child who exhibits persistent somatic complaints, very regressive behavior, significant school difficulties, severe anxieties including fear of leaving home even to go to school or visit friends, or any child who seems quite depressed or guilt-ridden, may need some time-limited professional support.

OUT OF THE MOUTHS OF BABES . . .

Several months ago, my seven-year-old niece, Nicole, and her nine-year-old brother, Justin, shared their own special brand of youthful wisdom with me on the subjects of death and grieving. Nicole and Justin are my youngest brother's children. At the time of this conversation, these two well-loved children had experienced the loss of only one grandparent so far in their young lives. Their deceased grandparent was my mother.

Recently I was out in California visiting my brother and his family. The kids and I were talking and playing outside. My visits usually set off some sort of convoluted conversation about how we are all related. Somehow the idea that their father was my baby brother or that their cousin, Jen, was my baby girl just tickles them silly.

Amidst the general confusion and laughter, Nicole asked me who my mother was and if she still took good care of me. I sadly but gently reminded her that my mother had been her grandmother and that she had died several years ago. I quickly reassured my softhearted young niece that since I was all grown up, I was now able to take care of myself.

But my niece was quick to remind me, *"You haven't lost your mother, she's right there in your heart,"* and she pointed to where she imagined my heart would be. Not to be outdone, my nephew added, *"Your mother doesn't have to be here to love you."* I don't know if Nicole and Justin truly understood the words that they were saying or if they were just repeating what their parents had taught them at the time of their grandmother's death. Either way, their words comforted me.

Chapter Ten

GRIEVING
ADOLESCENTS

*The good thing about being young is that you are not
experienced enough to know you cannot possibly
do the things you are doing.*

—AUTHOR UNKNOWN

RUNAWAY

Several months ago, I was driving past my hospital's emergency
room parking lot and briefly noticed an attractive, middle-
aged woman standing outside. She seemed to be yelling something, and other people, including a police officer, came in
and out of the ER doors to talk to her. Later that day, I heard
the story.

It seems that this woman's fifty-two-year-old husband had
awoken that morning feeling acutely ill. This man was otherwise healthy but clearly felt miserable that particular morning.
So his wife packed him and their fourteen-year-old daughter
into the car and drove to the hospital.

Tragically this woman's husband died of a massive heart attack within an hour of his arrival at the ER. Upon hearing this
unexpected and traumatic news, the young adolescent daughter

simply bolted from the hospital, ran outside, and disappeared from view. So this poor woman, who had barely absorbed the reality of her own status as a forty-nine-year-old widow, was now coping with a runaway teenager.

One might wonder, What was this young girl thinking? What was she trying to accomplish? How could she possibly be so selfish and hurtful toward her mother, at a time like this? Unfortunately, it is fairly typical for young adolescents to act impulsively. I don't believe that this particular teenager was trying to be hurtful. I doubt that she even thought about what destination she was running toward. I think this frightened child had simply fled a reality that was too scary to face. In running away, she temporarily postponed the need to confront and acknowledge her father's unexpected death. That reality was left behind in the hospital emergency room. Perhaps, subconsciously, she was also attempting to leave her father before he left her.

BIRTHDAY GIRL

Several years ago, a mentor of mine was diagnosed with thyroid cancer after only several weeks of vague and minor symptoms. Needless to say, the diagnosis came as a surprise. The doctors informed this middle-aged mental-health professional that the cancer had been caught early but that surgery and several months of outpatient treatment would still be needed. My efficient colleague went ahead and scheduled her operation before leaving the doctor's office and went home to calmly inform her husband and almost thirteen-year-old daughter of the diagnostic news and the upcoming surgical procedure.

The next day, I heard about this family conversation. My colleague had repeatedly reminded both her spouse and daughter that her cancer was quite treatable and most likely curable.

The surgery was very straightforward and the outpatient treatments, although inconvenient, would not be a great hardship. In fact, the surgery was already only two weeks away, and the treatments would most likely all be completed before the following summer's planned family vacation. Despite all of these reassurances, her daughter had burst into tears. Between sobs, the distraught teen cried out, "How could you do this to me? What about my birthday party? You said that you would help me. Everything was all planned, and now you've ruined it."

Inadvertently, my colleague had scheduled her surgery for the week before her daughter's thirteenth birthday party. Luckily, my friend was well informed on adolescent development and, although slightly taken aback, was not totally surprised by her child's egocentric response. Young teens are self-centered. In part, this is because they are so very self-conscious and unsure of themselves. So they spend a good bit of time worrying about what others are thinking about them. In this young girl's mind, the possibility of having to reschedule her all-important birthday party was tantamount to permanent social exile. Reading between the lines, however, we can also hear this young girl's fear of the unexpected and the implicit but unspoken "Who is going to take care of me, if you're sick?"

Ask the young. They know everything.

—Joseph Joubert,
French moralist (1754–1824)

Adolescence is a tumultuous chapter in the developmental journey from childhood to adulthood. In underdeveloped or tribal societies, the bridge between childhood and adulthood is often abrupt and ritualized. In industrialized countries, such as ours, the developmental limbo of adolescence can span almost ten years. Adolescents are neither adults nor children: They are somewhere in-between.

This is a challenging and confusing time for parents and teens alike. Teenagers usually develop quicker physiologically than they mature emotionally. Most teenagers will look like grown-ups long before they are capable of consistently thinking or acting like adults. Adolescents are searching for their own personal identity. They want to be unique. In other words, adolescents want to be something other than what they perceive their parents expect them to be. However, their early forays into self-definition and independence are cushioned by an overdependence upon peers for approval. They covet independence, but mistakenly view it as the ability to do as they please, not the capacity to be self-sufficient.

Adolescents can know a lot of facts but make horrible decisions. Their judgments are often based on short-term rewards versus long-term consequences. They also seem to falsely perceive themselves as invulnerable. Bad things happen to other people, but not to them. Most adolescents take risks that their parents wish they wouldn't. They do so in part because of peer pressure and in part because this risk-taking is a means of symbolically proving that they really aren't afraid of being on their own in the adult world. So, under the best of circumstances, adolescence represents a major developmental and family relationship challenge.

ADOLESCENT GRIEF

The death of a parent, sibling, or other loved one complicates this already confusing and intense developmental pathway. Unlike young children, adolescents are cognitively capable of understanding death. But that doesn't mean that they are emotionally prepared for it.

Adolescents want to be emancipated from the adults in their family system, but they don't want those adults to leave them. So losing a parent complicates this normal separation process. Friends are the security blankets for early and mid-stage adolescents. The need to fit in or belong is temporarily transitioned from the family to one's peer group. Having a seriously ill or dying sibling or parent makes a teen uncomfortably different from his or her peers. Similarly, a teen's friends often feel awkward around their grieving cohort and may distance themselves at a time when peer support is badly needed. Teenagers are trying to convince themselves that they are unafraid of the world outside the family doors, but serious illnesses and death threaten this developmental stance.

Unfortunately, when adolescents are frightened or overwhelmed, they often act angry or resentful instead of asking for help. Most teenagers work very hard to avoid looking either foolish or vulnerable, especially in front of their parents. So grieving teens might retreat to their room and close the door, even though they might in reality need a hug or a shoulder to cry on.

Grieving teens need comfort, just like children and adults do, but they are less likely to ask for it or to comfortably accept it.

Remember that there is no one right way to grieve, so teens need to be encouraged to grieve in their own way. They have a right to not talk when they don't feel comfortable doing so. Sometimes just sitting and watching television with other family

members is the level of contact or comfort needed. Opportunities to revisit positive memories, whether by looking at old
photo albums or sharing family stories, is often more palatable
than being pressured to share sad feelings.

Young teenagers tend to move in and out of grief. They are
visibly upset one moment, but acting perfectly normal with
their friends the next. This may be misperceived as uncaring
behavior, but it really just reflects the fact that adolescent grief
is different from adult grief. Some young teens seem upset at
the time of death, but then appear to quickly forget all about it.
This, too, can be disconcerting to the surrounding adults. But
often these youngsters will revisit their grief several weeks or
months later.

UNEXPECTED LOSS

Melanie was away from home at a high school track meet
when her mother suddenly collapsed and subsequently died from
a ruptured aneurysm before the ambulance could get her to the
hospital. Melanie came home to a changed family. She and her
older brother moved in with their maternal grandparents, as
their father worked longer hours to compensate for the loss of
his wife's income. Luckily, both Melanie and her brother were
able to stay at their same school and thus avoided the additional
losses of familiar surroundings, peers, and school activities.

For the first two weeks, Melanie was understandably distraught. She cried easily and often. She had difficulty sleeping
and concentrating at school. But supportive relatives, friends, and
teachers surrounded her, so eventually she quietly adapted to her
new motherless life. Six months later, Melanie asked her father if
she could "go talk to someone about Mom." Melanie explained
this request to me during our first therapy visit: "At first I was

upset, but mostly I was numb. It just felt so unreal. Everything was different. It was like my mom had gone on a business trip, but eventually she would come back, but then she didn't come back. I don't know why, but months after my mom's death, it all of a sudden hit me that this was real and she was never coming back. Then I started to cry all of the time and miss her like crazy."

Melanie was coping with the challenges of adolescent bereavement along with the challenges of a sudden, unexpected loss. This overwhelming, life-changing reality had come not only at an inconvenient developmental moment, but without warning or time to prepare. Melanie needed more time and more ongoing support to adjust to her mother's death and her significantly altered living situation.

Initially, Melanie had felt comfortable talking to her close friends and to her relatives about her mother's death. But eventually, it felt awkward to bring the subject up. Melanie didn't want her friends to think she was weird for still being upset some of the time, and she didn't want to upset her father or grandparents by bringing up the sad topic over and over again. So she kept her grief to herself.

With counseling, Melanie once again had a safe place to air her sadness. She also welcomed my recommendation to join a teenage support group for adolescents her own age who had recently lost a parent. Several family sessions allowed the adults in Melanie's family to give her permission to share her thoughts and sad feelings whenever she wanted to. Paradoxically, Melanie's relatives had been avoiding mentioning anything to do with Melanie's mother because they had been concerned about upsetting her or her brother. So the entire family recaptured an almost missed opportunity to grieve and reminisce together.

HELPFUL STRATEGIES

Most bookstores have a large selection of books for either children or adolescents who have lost a parent or grandparent. If your teen is a reader, the nice thing about a book is that it can be read in private. I usually recommend that newly bereaved families purchase several of these books to keep in an easily accessible place at home. That way young children can pull out the book and ask to have it read to them, and teens can simply take the book to their room if they choose to do so. The books that are written specifically for teens usually seek to normalize the situation and help grieving adolescents understand all of the confused emotions that they are experiencing.

If your teen isn't a reader, there may be other ways to help them express their feelings. Some teens find comfort in music; others write poetry. Some teens will benefit from taking an active part in the funeral service by doing a reading or writing a eulogy. Others will simply want to passively watch. A common grief-therapy exercise is to encourage the grieving adolescent to write a personal letter to the lost loved one. This provides a private opportunity to say anything that has been left unsaid. Like most children, teenagers benefit from opportunities to be involved in some kind of memorial activity for the deceased. Many teens also find it helpful to take part in an altruistic endeavor, such as raising money for breast cancer if you lost your loved one to breast cancer. Giving your adolescent a personal possession that once belonged to his or her lost loved one is another helpful idea.

Parents of grieving adolescents need to stay involved and connected despite their teenager's seeming ambivalence about their involvement. These parents need to find some way to say to their grieving offspring, "I'm here and I'm sorry that you're going through this. I know that you're confused, sad, and maybe even angry. So am I, but our family will get through this together. If you need to talk or have questions for me, I'll always be straight with you and we'll do the best we can to figure things out."

Support groups are also a helpful avenue for many grieving teens, not just Melanie. Many of today's local "grief centers" will have groups specifically designed for adolescents. These teen bereavement groups allow each youngster to know that he or she is not alone. In these groups, grieving teenagers get to meet others their own age in similar circumstances and with similar feelings. Many teens find it easier to talk to these fellow bereaved peers than to other friends who just "don't understand."

EXTRA HELP

Some teens are lucky enough to find a confidante and mentor in a special teacher, coach, youth-group leader, or younger member of their extended family. Some teens will need and benefit from the support of a professional counselor. Adolescents in general, with their developmental proclivity for impulsivity, experimentation, and risk-taking, are worth watching closely. This is particularly true for an adolescent who is also trying to negotiate an acute grief experience amidst all the other challenges and risks of the teenage years. Seeking extra help or support for a possibly troubled teen, whether grieving or not, should happen sooner rather than later.

Not all teens will need additional help to cope with bereavement, but some will. Any grieving teen who significantly withdraws from usual peer activities, who pursues excessive risk-taking behaviors (including promiscuity or drug experimentation), or who commits self-destructive acts even though they may seem only attention-seeking in nature (so-called suicidal gestures), needs and deserves extra help.

Other potential warning signs might include: notable weight changes in either direction, a social switch to a much older or "faster" peer group, a marked decline in the usual level of academic achievement, or a usually active and involved adolescent who now seems disinterested and exhausted almost all of the time. Teens who have struggled behaviorally or with depression prior to a loss in the family are certainly more likely to need and benefit from additional assistance. Then again, other teens will be upset and saddened by this family crisis but will also rally, grow, and mature impressively right before your eyes.

GROWING UP

When I was a boy of fourteen, my father was so ignorant that I could hardly stand to have the old man around.
But when I got to be twenty-one, I was astonished at how much the old man had learned in seven years.

—JOSH BILLINGS,
American humorist (1815–1885)

I recently went to a meeting at a local grief center. It was my first visit to this location. Both the physical setting and the staff members were warm and inviting. I spent a good deal of time talking to the director of this particular site. She is a compassionate and articulate woman who is clearly dedicated to easing bereavement pain whenever possible. Her center encourages its visitors to simply walk in off the street whenever they feel ready to talk to someone. Appointments are not necessary, since you can't always predict the moments you will be most in need of support. Grief is not considered an illness in this program but simply a fact of life that warrants extra comfort.

My conversation with the administrator of this special place lasted less than an hour. But it shifted quickly from our shared professional passions to our own personal experiences with grief. Lily had recently lost her mother, but her father had died when she was a young adolescent. My earliest experiences with grief were the cancer deaths of my three grandparents when I was only seventeen and away from home for the first time. Neither one of us thought it was an accident that we ended up doing the work that we now do and love. Sometimes the most difficult times in our lives can also be instructive and influential. Sometimes the most difficult times in our lives teach important lessons about the strengths that lie inside each of us.

If we are lucky, the difficult times of our youth will shape us in ways that are healthy, healing, and meaningful.

PART THREE

Special
Challenges

Chapter Eleven

SUDDEN, UNEXPECTED LOSSES

Death leaves a heartache no one can heal,
love leaves a memory no one can steal.

—AUTHOR UNKNOWN

DIFFERENT LOSSES MEAN DIFFERENT CHALLENGES

There are many different ways to lose a loved one. None of them are easy. None of them are pain-free. But different types of losses present different bereavement challenges. For example, loved ones of someone who is seriously ill must bear witness to their beloved's sad journey from health through life-threatening illness. They may watch their loved one struggle and suffer. They will need to cope with the heartrending juggling act of supporting their loved one while simultaneously attending to their own pain and fear. They will lose their family member piece by piece over the course of whatever illness is winning the war.

Those who experience an expected loss will, however, have time to prepare. They will have the opportunity to attend to any unfinished business. They will have the chance to say "I love you" and time to say good-byes. This time of preparation is called anticipatory grieving. It does not make the grieving that comes after your loss any easier, but it does give you a bit of a head start on the mourning work ahead.

Those who grieve sudden, unexpected losses have no warning. There is no time to prepare. Their loved one was here one moment and literally gone forever the next. There was no time for any conversation, much less one involving good-bye. Life has changed in the blink of an eye, or in the time it takes to answer the phone.

Sudden deaths also come in many forms. They are often the outcome of a tragic motor vehicle accident. But they can also be the end result of a violent crime, a suicide, or an unanticipated medical catastrophe such as a massive heart attack or stroke. Sudden, unanticipated deaths can also be part of the devastation left behind after such natural disasters as fires, floods, or hurricanes. Sudden losses can involve one lost life or many. Sudden, unexpected losses shake our illusions of control and safety to the core.

THE UNANTICIPATED PHONE CALL

Cheryl is a fifty-three-year-old bank teller with a ready smile and a friendly word for each and every one of her customers at the bank. I am one of those customers, and Cheryl's ability to remember her regular customers' names and also something personal about each of them constantly impresses me. Because of Cheryl, going to the bank is like visiting an old friend instead of just conducting a piece of impersonal business. But underneath that friendly, welcoming demeanor is a woman coping with the grief of sudden loss.

Cheryl is no stranger to the challenges left behind after a sudden, unanticipated death. She is also familiar with the grief that follows the expected loss of a seriously ill family member. When Cheryl was five years old, she lost her biological father to a car accident. Her mother eventually remarried, and for a long while all was well. In February 2005, Cheryl's brother died after a six-year battle with colon cancer. He was only forty-six years old. In April 2008, Cheryl's mother, who had been suffering from bronchitis, collapsed at home. The ambulance crew came quickly and was able to resuscitate her. But Cheryl's mom had unexpectedly suffered a massive heart attack and was declared brain dead at the hospital. Several days later, the family agreed to have her life support discontinued. And then, in April 2009, one year after her mother's sudden death, Cheryl unexpectedly lost her husband of twenty-seven years.

Cheryl's husband, Jay, was eleven years her senior and a longtime sufferer of asthma and chronic obstructive pulmonary disease (COPD). For many years Jay had been a strong, active man. He had been a veteran, an auto-body mechanic, a truck driver, and a volunteer firefighter. But then his chronic illnesses caught up with him and he became more and more disabled, and he eventually retired. Jay never complained as he struggled to breathe, becoming weaker and more fatigued.

But hope was seemingly around the corner. First, Jay was evaluated for a lung transplant. When this opportunity didn't come to pass, Cheryl and Jay were very disappointed. But then a second opportunity arose—a surgical procedure that was to provide significant relief. Jay went through the surgery without any untoward signs of distress. The evening after his successful operation, Cheryl was visiting Jay in his hospital room. The doctors were pleased with his progress and so was she. Jay was awake and alert. They talked quietly, grateful for the better days ahead. Eventually they kissed good night, and Jay sent Cheryl home to get some sleep.

Cheryl returned to work the next day, planning to visit Jay that evening after work. And then the unexpected phone call came. The phone call was so unexpected that initially Cheryl didn't understand what the hospital physician was trying to tell her. "I guess that I just didn't hear her or just couldn't accept what she was saying. I thought she was asking me to sign some papers and I kept trying to explain that I would be in later that afternoon. But finally she got my attention by saying, 'You need to sit down now and listen to what I am telling you, because you are not hearing me. I am so very sorry but . . .' All of a sudden, I guess I heard what she was trying to tell me. I think that I screamed and dropped the phone. I wanted to call my mother, but then I remembered that she was dead."

Jay had suffered an uncommon postoperative complication and died before Cheryl could get to the hospital. "He was just gone. It never occurred to me it could happen like this. I wish I had stayed at the hospital that night." Cheryl went through the next days and weeks in a daze. She doesn't remember much of the funeral, other than it was with full military honors, which was a comfort to her and something her Jay deserved.

Cheryl has only been widowed for a few months, so she is still coping with the very early stages of acute grief. Her bereavement is complicated by the unexpected nature of her loss. So the shock and disbelief still linger. It still bothers her to not know for sure what happened or why. She refused an autopsy at the time, but now wonders if she should have decided differently. She finds herself looking for Jay when she gets home after work. Sometimes she thinks that she can see him sitting in his favorite chair. Cheryl shakes her head in disbelief, commenting, "Who ever would have thought that my stepfather and I would become widowed in the same year?" This disconcerting experience of prolonged disbelief and questioning is common among those who are grieving an unexpected loss.

Cheryl is finding her own path through the early months of widowhood, despite the lack of warning or time for preparation that has accompanied her most recent loss. She visits the cemetery regularly. She wants Jay to know that she is OK, because he would want to know, and telling him so makes her feel better. She has met with a financial planner in order to better understand her current situation. For now, Cheryl finds that it is best for her to keep most things the same. She is keeping Jay's beloved truck and maintaining the garden he helped create. In the evening she listens to the oldies music that she and Jay once enjoyed together. She embraces her memories of her good, kind, and giving husband. She wears his wedding ring on a gold chain around her neck. Cheryl is grateful for all of her supportive neighbors, friends, and family members. She feels fortunate that among her acquaintances are four other women who have been widowed within the last two years. "It helps to compare notes with other women who are going through the same thing. We all agree to take it one day at a time." Cheryl knows firsthand about grief, so she understands that time is on her side during the long road of healing that lies ahead.

Hope is grief's best music.

—AUTHOR UNKNOWN

THE UNIMAGINABLE CAN HAPPEN

Linda is an accountant. She is a bright, capable woman with a lovely smile and a wry sense of humor. Like Cheryl, Linda's loss experience began with an unanticipated phone call. Unlike

Cheryl, Linda's unexpected tragedy occurred years ago. In the early morning of a day that started out like any other, Linda's mother received a phone call. The stranger on the other end informed Linda's mom that her son Ray's Maryland home was on fire and that the situation was grave.

Ray was the only member of the family living out of state. Linda's mother, father, and married brother, Paul, were all nearby. One year earlier, Ray had married Marie. Both he and Marie had been previously married and then divorced and they each had two young children from their prior marriages. This newly-wed couple had worked hard and thoughtfully on the blending of their preexisting families. And that hard work had seemingly paid off; they were very happy together.

Linda's distraught mother called her daughter immediately after receiving the frightening phone call. Linda called her brother Paul and his expectant wife. Then they all held their breath, waiting to confirm or disprove the unsettling message delivered by a total stranger. Perhaps this was some kind of mistake or sick joke? Sadly, Ray's mother-in-law called shortly after to confirm the news. She was there at the site of the fire, and it was horrible. Linda and her parents hurriedly threw belongings into suitcases and made the four-and-a-half-hour drive to their loved one's now smoldering home. Brother Paul waited at home; his wife was due with their third child.

Linda remembers how, even in the very beginning, they each handled the situation differently. Her mother became confused and forgetful, her father calm and in charge. Linda's mind was sharp, but her emotions were absent. She just couldn't grasp what was happening. It was so very surreal.

Nothing could have prepared them for what they encountered when they arrived at Ray's home. There was smoke damage everywhere. The front of the house was intact, but the back was a blackened shell. The house was cordoned off, but there were firefighters, police, media people, and hundreds of spectators surrounding the burned home. It had been a five-alarm fire and had lasted only six minutes, but those six minutes had cost six lives. Ray, Marie, and their four children ranging in age from six to twelve were all gone.

Linda's family was forced to deal not only with one sudden, unexpected loss, but with multiple losses that had occurred simultaneously. Their initial introduction to grief was also part and parcel of a public spectacle. Over the next several days Ray's front yard was covered with candles, flowers, and other memorial items left by total strangers. The media covered the funeral service held three days later. There was television coverage of the six caskets and various family members coming and going from the church.

Linda describes the very public nature of this private loss as adding to the shock they all experienced at that time. "It was all so unreal and so very overwhelming. Total strangers were crying and carrying on: It just didn't make any sense." "Overwhelming" is a word Linda uses a lot when describing this early time as they all struggled to process the unimaginable tragedy placed unexpectedly at their family doorstep.

In addition to the scope, suddenness, and public nature of this loss experience, Linda's family faced other challenges. The six caskets were closed. There were no intact bodies to recover, so that avenue of closure and finality was not open to them. Additionally, the nature of these losses raised unsettling issues regarding fault and control. Was there someone at fault for this devastating house fire? Ray had been a "safety freak," so if something like this could happen to him, it could happen to anyone. Ultimately the fire was declared an unfortunate accident, but the investigation took ten months and involved multiple detailed reports that Linda's family needed to read and digest, causing them to revisit the horror of the fire over and over again.

Days later, Linda and her family returned home, still trying to process what had just occurred. They held a private memorial service for family and close friends a week later, to seek the solace and support that had been lacking in the prior publicity-ridden ritual. Linda and her mother went to several bereavement support groups, but then decided on private counseling instead. Their private grief had been too public already.

Linda's family created other rituals to help memorialize their many losses. Each year around the anniversary of the fire, Linda and her mother meet Ray's mother-in-law at the cemetery. They weed, place new flowers, reminisce about Ray, Marie, and the children. And then they leave, go have lunch, and talk about the present and the future.

Because of the public nature of this family tragedy, money started pouring in from empathetic strangers. Linda's family has chosen to contribute these funds to memorial efforts that their lost children would have appreciated. So a camping scholarship has been established through the Boy Scouts; books were contributed to one school in need, and a playground was refurbished for another. And of course money was contributed to a children's hospital burn unit, in the hopes that others would be more fortunate than Ray and his family. Linda views this "re-gifting" as Ray's legacy. Ray was an amazing father, and he loved doing things with kids.

Today, Linda declares that her family is in a better place. But it wasn't easy. And some days it still isn't. Linda's mother still can't stand the smell of smoke without feeling ill. Linda's dad had nightmares for quite a while. Linda and her family still struggle at "anniversary time." Years later, the anniversary of the fire is still a challenging time for each of them. It is easier than it once was, but "anniversary time" is still a sadder, turning-inward time of year.

Linda's parents had heard about the reportedly high divorce rate among parents who lose children, so they worked hard to make sure this wouldn't happen. They understood and accepted that they would each grieve differently. Linda, the accountant, no longer balances her checkbook. She just rounds it up. Her perspective about what is really important has changed in many ways. Opportunities to say "I love you" are never missed. Special family events, such as birthdays, are a priority now: Nothing is more important. The special friends who hung in during the worst of times are not just appreciated but treasured.

I asked Linda for her advice to others who might go through a similarly overwhelming family catastrophe. She shared, "You may feel stuck or frozen in time for days, months, or even years, but it does get better. Life will be different, though. You can't go back to the way it was before. Your life has to move in a new direction somehow. Our family is now stronger and closer. We've changed in good ways. We're much more involved with each other and with others in the community. We each did it differently, but we each found our own way through the grief. And we don't take anything for granted. Moments are treasured. I try to remember that it can always be worse, so I count my blessings. You can't let yourself go and stay in that little black hole, you have to find something, anything, to appreciate."

SUDDEN DEATH'S SPECIAL OBSTACLES

Cheryl's and Linda's stories depict many of the special challenges and obstacles those grieving an unexpected loss may have to face. Remember, grieving a sudden, unexpected loss is different from grieving a loss that has been anticipated. It is not better or worse, just different. For example, both women reported a prolonged sense of shock or disbelief. This delay in acute mourning is the understandable by-product of a lack of any warning or time to prepare. It can be likened to an emotional jet lag. Eventually, this surreal sensation will dissipate, but it will take a while.

Like Cheryl, many relatives who lose their loved ones to a sudden health-related circumstance will have to make both autopsy decisions and funeral arrangements while they are still dazed and barely able to process the life-altering events that are unfolding around them. And of course, Cheryl's wish that she had stayed at the hospital that last night speaks to the lost opportunity to say a meaningful good-bye.

Linda's family tragedy graphically depicts the challenges and complexities involved in experiencing multiple losses simultaneously and without warning. Accidental deaths also raise so many other issues that must be dealt with in the midst of an intense grieving process. The investigations, the publicity, the financial complexities, and the need to grapple with the senselessness of these deaths are all overwhelming hurdles to be overcome. Perhaps the most difficult challenge involves the struggle to make peace with the fact that your loved one was lost simply because of being in the wrong place at the wrong time.

Other forms of sudden death each add their own special obstacles to the mourning work ahead. Those who lose their loved one to a violent crime often have to deal with the added challenges of prolonged legal proceedings and the possibility that the perpetrator may never come to justice. And how does one quiet the unbidden imaginings of the last moments of a loved one's life, regardless of whether he or she was a murder victim or lost in fire, flood, or violent storm? Large-scale disasters such as airplane crashes often involve a delay in identification of the dead and the need to travel to an unknown, impersonal location to await the news of your loved one's fate.

Surviving the suicide of a loved one means confronting the unfortunate but very real stigma attached to this type of loss. Comfort and sympathy, sadly, may be less forthcoming. Because of societal misconceptions, you will have to decide what you choose to share regarding the circumstances of your loved one's sudden demise. And there are so many unanswered questions left behind after a suicidal death. The biggest of these questions is "Why?" And that unanswered question leaves its own legacy of guilt, anger, and the need to cope with unsettling feelings of betrayal and rejection as you also mourn a loss. But your loss is real, and most commonly it is the by-product of a disease and a good deal of suffering on the part of your lost loved one. Whether that disease was depression, substance abuse, or perhaps a combination of both, the pain that it caused your loved one and is now causing you is real and undeserved.

These very real challenges add to the complexity and intensity of mourning following a sudden, unexpected loss. Because of all of these issues, sudden, unanticipated losses usually leave fairly intense grief reactions in their wake. Early on, there may be more denial and questioning. Later there may be a prolonged struggle to make sense of these losses and make peace with what often seem to be unpredictable and unacceptable circumstances.

COPING STRATEGIES FOR SUDDEN LOSS

Cheryl's and Linda's stories also depicted some of the positive coping strategies that others experiencing similarly traumatic, unexpected losses might find helpful. Cheryl's intuitive inclination to keep many aspects of her life the same for the short term is a way of giving herself time to catch up with the new realities of her life. For now, there will be comfort in familiar things and activities. She is aware that possibly down the road it may make sense to sell Jay's truck, but not now. Cheryl's decision to meet with a financial advisor sooner as opposed to later also made sense within the context of her unanticipated instant widowhood. Most important, for now Cheryl is choosing to take it one day at a time and focusing on doing the things that comfort or help her in some way. She is being patient with herself. She is being kind to herself. And she should.

Linda's family's decision to have a second private funeral service after the first, very public, service was an important early step in their long healing process. Grief is a personal and private journey, and they needed to find support and solace from those who would truly feel connected to them and their loss. This family's thoughtful approach to memorializing Ray and his family (the school books, the school playground, the Boy Scout scholarship, the burn-unit donation) has benefited many others but has also helped them to find meaning and purpose in their loss.

The annual cemetery trip is another positive means of memorializing and remembering. It gives ongoing grief its own time and place. This ritual also allows the two families, each of which has lost a child and several grandchildren, to comfort each other. It is worth noting that in the aftermath of other disasters involving multiple losses and multiple families, it is not uncommon for the surviving family members to meet annually as an ongoing memorial service to their shared lost loved ones.

Linda's parents worked hard on their marriage after the loss of their son, daughter-in-law, and grandchildren. They gave each other room to grieve in their own fashion and avoided a schism that might have otherwise developed. Lastly, Linda and her mother did choose to seek private counseling, while others in the family did not. Because of the intensity and complex obstacles involved in bereavement from sudden, unexpected losses, many individuals will find either a support group or a private counselor a helpful means of coping with the challenges they face.

The bottom line in both Cheryl's and Linda's stories is that time can heal. Cheryl senses that and Linda knows it. Sudden, unexpected losses take our breath away. For a while, we lose the illusion we once held of a safe, predictable world. We are lost and not sure that we want to be found. But slowly, gradually, you will find your way through the confusion and pain. It will get better, and eventually there will be reasons to treasure life and those who are still around you.

The goals of grief, whether anticipated or not, are to survive, to accept, to remember, and to find a way to move forward into whatever your new life has to offer you.

Chapter Twelve

THE LOSS OF A CHILD

I Am Not There

Do not stand at my grave and weep,
I am not there. I do not sleep.
I am a thousand winds that blow,
I am the snow on the mountain's rim,
I am the sand at the water's edge,
I am the sunlight on ripened grain,
I am the gentle autumn rain,
When you awaken in the morning's hush,
I am the swift uplifting rush of quiet birds in circled flight,
I am the star that shines at night,
Do not stand at my grave and cry,
I am not there, I did not die.

—MARY ELIZABETH FRYE

Almost everyone I have either worked with or spoken to has agreed that losing a child is the most difficult of all losses to bear. This sentiment has been expressed by those who have lost a child and by those who have not. The reasons for this shared perception are fairly straightforward. There is nothing existentially acceptable about losing a child. They are meant to outlive us. The death of a child before his or her parents violates our belief in the predictability and continuity of the life cycle. This heartbreaking sense of unnatural discontinuity exists whether we are talking about the death of an infant, a young child, an older child, or even an adult child.

Our children represent not only our past and present but also our future. Our children and their children are both our legacy and our small piece of eternity. So when parents lose a child, they are also losing a piece of themselves, in ways that are both real and symbolic. When a child dies, his or her parents also lose the future they believed was that child's birthright. One must learn to accept all of the things that your lost child will never have or get to do—all of the developmental milestones, such as graduations and weddings, which you will not get to witness. Even the loss of an unborn child through miscarriage triggers the need to grieve for what was just beginning along with all that was yet to be.

In a world that made sense, all children would be protected and nurtured. Children are our most vulnerable and precious resource. They are innocents. They should be sheltered from harm. So witnessing the struggles of a seriously ill child or grieving the loss of a child, whether due to illness or accident, challenges all of us to make peace with a painfully unpalatable reality.

For all of these reasons, and many more, bereavement following the loss of a child tends to be prolonged and intense. The death of a child can be either sudden and unexpected or long anticipated. Accidents are the more common source of childhood mortality, but chronic illnesses such as asthma, cancer, depression, diabetes, muscular dystrophy, and cystic fibrosis also take the lives of some of our youth. In any circumstance, the loss of a child forces the bereaved family and all those who know them to confront and make peace with a possibility that none of us wants to acknowledge.

UNFINISHED BUSINESS

Steven was diagnosed with muscular dystrophy when he was five years old, but his parents had suspected it years earlier. Muscular dystrophy is a genetically transmitted disease whose primary symptom is progressive muscle degeneration. These kids are otherwise healthy, intelligent, and loving. They are not sick per se, but they become increasingly disabled over time and usually die at relatively young ages.

Muscular dystrophy ran in Steven's mother's family, so Steven's parents sought genetic counseling prior to conception. They were told that there was a fifty-fifty chance that a child of theirs would have muscular dystrophy. They considered adoption, but ultimately decided that they would love their biological child no matter what. Four years after they married, Steven's parents had two sons within nineteen months of each other. The older did not have muscular dystrophy; the younger, Steven, did.

Steven was born in 1963. At that time, there were few resources available for families with disabled children. There were no support groups for parents of children with muscular dystrophy in their city. There was no special education department set up to deal with the needs of physically disabled schoolchildren at the school that Steven attended. And so his mother learned how to take care of her special-needs child, and she learned how to become an advocate for her own child and other disabled children.

Steven's mother also grieved as her child struggled with his chronic illness. "You grieve when they are alive, and you grieve again when they die." The earliest signs of Steven's illness, including slowed speech, were evident before his diagnosis at age five. By age eleven, Steven was in a wheelchair. And yet despite increasing levels of disability, Steven graduated high school and began attending a local community college. He was studying accounting. Steven was twenty-one years old and weighed only sixty pounds at the time of his death.

I never met Steven, but I have seen childhood pictures of him. He was slender, with dark hair, dark eyes, and a smile that lit up his entire face. Despite his visible suffering, he seemed to have the capacity to find moments of true joy. He must have been an amazing young man. Steven's mother shares her son's attractive facial features and his smile. She is a strong, resourceful woman; she is a survivor.

Steven's mother readily admits to the relief that she initially felt after Steven's death. Steven had died at home, after several days of increasing difficulty swallowing and breathing. So, at first, the strongest emotion was relief that his suffering was over. And the horrible pressure cooker of waiting for the next medical crisis was also over. But then there was grief. This grief was for the child lost, but also for all the things that he would never get to do. "There is such a sense of incompleteness, of unfinished business."

Steven's mother sought grief counseling initially through the local Visiting Nurses Association because they had helped care for Steven at home. Later she worked with professional counselors. Steven's parents' marriage faltered and failed a short time after his death. Steven's mother doesn't believe that their son's death was the only reason for the eventual divorce, but it didn't help.

Steven's mother describes her journey through grief as a

"gradual process." She says, "Very slowly, the pain goes from your eyeballs to your baby left toe, via your throat, your heart, and the pit of your stomach. But eventually, one day at a time, it gets better. The pain is reduced from overwhelming acute discomfort to a manageable memory and it becomes a part of who you are. It's just there; it doesn't go away, but it doesn't stop you from holding on to the good memories or living your life."

WHEN THE SKY FALLS

Jessie was fifteen when she was diagnosed with depression. Depression, although classified as a psychiatric disorder, is also a biological disorder that runs in families. And there were relatives on both sides of Jessie's family who had suffered from depression. So despite an intact and loving family, and a lovely home, Jessie began her struggle with depression. She went to several different therapists and she was put on several different antidepressant medications. Each one helped for a while, but then the engulfing fatigue, unhappiness, and hopelessness returned once more. Jessie struggled to keep up her school grades, which were once almost perfect. Unlike other depressed adolescents, Jessie did not self-medicate with alcohol or other substances, but she did withdraw from many of her usual social and extracurricular activities. Luckily, several close friends hung in and called or stopped by often, but many others did not.

Many depressive illnesses respond well and reasonably quickly to a combined approach of medication and therapy. But sometimes adolescent depression takes a bit longer to treat. Finally after several months of parental angst and Jessie's silent, withdrawn suffering, it appeared that Jessie was starting to feel better.

She was more animated, and every once in a while her parents could see glimpses of "the old Jessie" in her smile and humor. Jessie had recently been started on a new medication and she seemed to be responding more favorably than previously. Her parents felt like they could breathe again, after months of holding their breath. Jessie started to go out with friends again. The sadness and tension that had invisibly taken hold in their family home started to subside. Gradually, thankfully, life returned to normal.

Jessie graduated with honors from high school and planned to start college the upcoming fall. She wanted to study psychology. In early August, Jessie and several friends were driving to a local amusement park for an afternoon outing. An inebriated driver, who was in the process of running a red light, sideswiped their car. Jessie was killed instantly; her two friends were seriously injured but eventually recovered.

Jessie's parents were visited at home by a local police officer whose sad duty it was to inform them of their child's tragic car accident and unexpected death. Jessie's mother fell to the ground as her shell-shocked husband tried to cushion her fall. For several moments after the police officer left, they were unable to speak or to move. In less than three minutes, the sky had fallen at their feet. They had lost their beloved daughter. And because Jessie had been an only child, they had lost their job as parents, long before they were prepared to do so.

Like so many others coping with a sudden, unanticipated loss, Jessie's parents went through the next several days and weeks in a fog of dazed disbelief. Eventually this dazed disbelief alternated with waves of acute distress. Mourning is not just an emotional experience; it is a physical experience as well. Both of Jessie's parents had difficulty sleeping for several months. Jessie's mother reports that her arms actually hurt, as she ached to hold her daughter just one more time. Jessie's father often sighed, as if he couldn't quite get enough air to breathe. They each cried, but at different times.

Early on, Jessie's parents learned that they couldn't effectively console each other. Neither one of them could cope with the other's pain, because their own pain was so intense and overwhelming. And so they each grieved differently and separately. But accepting this surprising marital reality freed them up to support each other in other ways. Each could tell when the other was having a "bad grief day," and would make allowances accordingly.

They each also coped differently. Jessie's father was a newspaperman, so he read others' stories of loss and he wrote his own. He wrote daily entries in a personal journal, and he wrote an article for a local newspaper in the hopes that others might benefit from what he was learning about grief and surviving the loss of a child.

Jessie's mom needed different outlets for her grief. She needed to keep moving and she needed to talk about it. So she joined a gym and a local walking club. She went into individual therapy for a while, later joining a support group for bereaved mothers. Jessie's parents understood and appreciated these differences in their respective coping styles. And so when he was having a bad day, she would encourage him to go "talk to his journal." And when she was having a sad day, he would encourage her to go out to the gym for a while. And so together, they survived the early months of their grief.

GIVE YOURSELF PERMISSION

Becoming a parent is so much more than merely adding a new relationship to your life. Becoming a parent is a life-altering experience. It changes both who you are and what you do. Parenting is a full-time job with no vacations or days off. Parenthood also changes how you define yourself. For years, I introduced myself in the neighborhood that my kids grew up in as "Jay or Jen's mom." And that was all I needed to say; everybody knew who I was.

Like widowhood, the challenges of parental bereavement extend far beyond the unfathomable loss of a loved one. The loss of a child can involve changes and adjustments in almost every aspect of your daily life. If the lost child was still living at home, there will be his or her room and possessions to contend with. Your daily schedule will change in big and little ways, including how many people you now cook dinner for on a nightly basis.

If your child was living outside the home, then whatever the usual routine was for phone contact, e-mail communications, and regular visitations will all be achingly disrupted. If your child was married with children, then your relationship with the now-widowed spouse and your grandchildren may be altered in ways you are either comfortable with or not.

Regardless of the age of your deceased child, there will be holidays, birthdays, and so on to cope with. There will also be the graduations and weddings or other special occasions of their peers that will further signify all that has been lost, because you have not just lost your child's present but his or her hoped-for future as well. Over time, you will find your way through each of these adaptations. The first year will probably not be the easiest, but each year you will have a new opportunity to sort out new routines and rituals, along with ways to hold on to, remember, and memorialize your lost child.

There are no rules about "the right way" to deal with your child's room or how to best celebrate the first holidays without your child. Eventually it will be possible to be both happy for your friends' children's celebrations and good fortune and yet sad regarding what your own child has missed out on. But initially, you may choose to decline invitations to these events because they will be too painful for you. Give yourself permission to do what you can and accept that it is the best you can do right now. That doesn't mean that next month or next year you might not want to do things differently.

SOCIAL ISSUES

Parenthood also alters your social life. If you are a parent, then you tend to know and befriend other parents with similar-aged children. If you have children at home, then their friends usually become frequent visitors to your home and at your dinner table. So parenthood is not just about one's family status, it is a lifestyle. Parental bereavement doesn't just drastically alter your family life; it may affect your social existence as well.

For example, will you stay friends with the other parents with similar-aged children to the one you have lost? Will you continue to befriend your lost child's friends? Your friends with like-aged children will also struggle with this issue. Can they talk to you about their child's accomplishments without hurting or upsetting you? After all, before your child's death, talking about each other's kids was what you did every day. But now what happens?

These social issues take time to sort out. Good friends will take their cues from you. If you don't ask about their children, then at least for a while they will be sensitive to your pain and not share news about your lost child's friends who have survived and continue to thrive. Eventually, though, if some of these friendships are truly important to you and you want to sustain them, you will need to find a way to allow your friends to share that part of their lives with you again.

When you have lost a child, eventually you will meet new people who do not know your personal history and they will ask the seemingly innocent questions "Do you have children?" and "How many children do you have?" These simple questions can be complicated for the bereaved parent. Some bereaved parents choose to share with anyone who asks about the child they have lost, as well as about any surviving children. Others decide not to disclose this emotion–laden information, at least not during early conversations with new acquaintances. There is no right or wrong answer, but if you are a newly bereaved parent, it might help to think about this issue before you confront it. And then do whatever is most comfortable for you.

Over time your social network may shift, but it shouldn't fall apart. Truly good friends will weather the storm with you. Perhaps others will not. You also may find new friends over time, whether they are other bereaved parents who understand your journey through grief or others you have met because of new activities or interests that you have added to your life. Be patient with yourself and with others. Most of your friends probably don't feel especially prepared to deal with these awkward social issues. They want to comfort you but may not know how. Good friends are worth both the extra time and the extra effort.

FAMILY ISSUES

Meanwhile, as you are coping with your own grief along with all of the big and little changes in your daily life and social existence, there are still family dynamics to attend to. How is your spouse or partner doing, if you have one? How are your parents, your child's grandparents, doing? And if you have other children, how are the surviving siblings of your deceased child doing? What do each of these people need from you or from others? How do you help your other children when you can barely negotiate your own grief?

Most bereaved parents I have worked with eventually look back and painfully acknowledge that they do not think they were able to provide enough emotional support for their deceased child's surviving but grieving siblings. I am always touched by the courageous honesty of this self-reflection. Even in this instance, grief may be a collective family experience, but it is also a private, personal journey.

The role of the surviving sibling or siblings is not an easy one. There will be remorse for things said or not said, and things done or not done. There will be the guilt inherent in having survived when a brother or sister did not. And there will be the hurt and confusion that inevitably comes when bearing witness to the parental pain that your mere presence as a surviving child is not sufficient to overcome.

These sibling issues are important to deal with, but it is unrealistic to think that an acutely grieving parent can accomplish all of this without help from others. Whether you choose to enlist the help of extended family members to spend extra time with your surviving child or children, or you locate a local support group, or you consider private counseling, please once again give yourself permission to consider any and all of these options. The goal is to get your surviving children the help and support that they may need to accomplish their sibling grief work. The goal is not for you to prove that you can super-parent even under the direst circumstances.

Similarly, parental bereavement is a time to consider outside assistance sooner rather than later. If your marriage was already stressed or compromised in some way, then couples counseling would be most useful to you before you experience a total marital breakdown. Parental bereavement understandably carries with it an increased risk of not just marital strain but also individual wear and tear. It will be important for you to try to keep yourself healthy. So even though you don't feel like it, try to get enough sleep, eat right, exercise, and check in with your regular physician so that your health status can be monitored during the initial months or year of acute grief.

If you have a family history of depression or a personal history of depression, or if your grief seems both unbearable and unending, then consider an evaluation with a professional therapist or psychiatrist to make sure your grief is not transitioning into a depressive episode as well. Grief is hard enough, but grief and depression at the same time clearly warrant extra help.

This may also be the time to consider several sessions of family counseling. That way the differing experiences and needs of parents, surviving children, and perhaps even grandparents can be safely shared and worked on. After the loss of a family's child, everyone in the family is hurting and trying to figure out how to get his or her own needs met along with how best to support or at least not upset other family members. This can get awfully confusing and cumbersome at times. In this instance, an experienced family therapist can be a powerful and effective mediator, helping the family to find its way through the emotional morass of individual and family grief.

FOREVER

Once you become a parent, you stay a parent to your children no matter how old they or you get. Whether your child is two or forty-two, you are still the parent and he or she is still your child, albeit your grown child. The nature of the relationship may change, but the emotional ties that bind you remain. I believe that our children will always be a part of our lives, and ourselves, whether they are living in the bedroom upstairs or married and living out of state or no longer alive. As the poem that started this chapter implies, our children are and will always be a part of our world, whether they are physically present or not. It is my hope for anyone who grieves the loss of a child that time will soften the pangs of your sorrow and that with time your memories and a sense of enduring connection will rise up to comfort you.

There is no grief that time does not lessen and soften.

—CICERO

Chapter Thirteen

A CAREGIVER'S GRIEF

Love begins by taking care of the closest ones
—the ones at home.

—Mother Teresa

IN SICKNESS AND IN HEALTH . . .

Andrew is a fifty-eight-year-old business executive. He has worked for the same company for more than thirty years, and last year he was in line for a major promotion. Andrew had hoped to stay with his current employer until his expected retirement at age sixty-five, at which point he and his wife of thirty-five years, Beverly, had plans to travel across the United States. Both Andrew and Beverly were Pennsylvania-born and raised, and had never left the tri-state area.

This devoted married couple had no children, but they did have a large network of good friends and an active social life. Andrew and Beverly were hard workers (she worked as an executive secretary for a downtown law firm), but they also shared many outside interests. They were avid bowlers, card players, and ballroom dancers. A year ago, both would have said life was good and hopefully only going to get better.

But then, unexpectedly, Andrew had a major, debilitating

stroke. One minute Andrew was on his way out to play golf with his cronies; an hour later Beverly received the phone call informing her that he had collapsed on the golf course and had been taken by ambulance to a nearby emergency facility. Thankfully, he survived.

But a month later, after two weeks in the hospital and another two weeks in a rehabilitation unit, Andrew came home a changed man. The strong, vibrant, and always-in-control man Beverly had married was gone, and in his place was someone familiar yet not known. Andrew came home in a wheelchair. He was unable to walk without assistance. His speech was garbled and he often seemed confused or disoriented, requiring repeated instructions to accomplish even the simplest tasks. He became frustrated easily; impatient both with himself and with Beverly when she tried to help him. The lifestyle and relationship that Andrew and Beverly had known and enjoyed had disappeared, leaving behind challenges neither had anticipated.

Beverly chose to keep Andrew at home instead of following her physician's recommendation that he be placed in a long-term-care facility. "Andrew in a nursing home. Never! He'd never allow that to happen to me." Fortunately, Andrew's long-standing employer chose to put him on an extended medical leave and retain his health benefits. However, this generous arrangement still meant a significant cut in Andrew's salary. Additionally, Beverly had to cut back on her work hours in order to care for her now-disabled spouse. Initially, good friends came over to "watch" Andrew when Beverly had to go to work, but eventually she had to hire outside caretakers to supplement her own spousal caregiving efforts.

Six months into this new life, Beverly's family physician sent her to see me. Beverly had lost weight and appeared understandably exhausted and dejected. Her physician was concerned about depression, a reportedly common occurrence among family caregivers. Beverly, although thin-looking with dark circles under her eyes, was still an attractive woman. During our first session there were fleeting glimpses of the vivacious, happy person she had reportedly been prior to her husband's stroke. "If someone had told me six months ago that this was going to be my life, I'm not sure I would have believed them," she claimed when we first met.

"I feel like I'm grieving all of the time. I'm grieving for the husband that I've lost, even though he's still there. But he was my best friend. We could talk about anything. And we never argued. Now we still talk, but it's not the same. His speech is better, but it's still hard for him to express himself. He used to be so quick and so funny. I was the serious one; he always made me smile. Now, because he's so frustrated all of the time, well, he gets so annoyed. I just can't please him. I can't make this all right for him or for me. But the hardest part is seeing my husband, this proud man, suffer all of these indignities and I can't protect him from that. But I wish that I could."

Beverly continued, "I miss the wonderful life that we shared. We belonged to a couples bowling league, a couples card circle, and we danced every weekend. That's all gone now. And our friendships seem to be fading away also. I'm either at work or I'm at home taking care of Andrew, but mostly I'm alone. Occasionally friends still call, but I'm too tired to go anywhere. And I can't go anywhere without finding someone to stay with Andrew. Luckily my brother comes over and stays with him one evening a week so that I can go food shopping and run some other errands. I guess I'm also grieving for the future that we had naively assumed was ahead. Last week, I started to clean out our travel drawer and throw away all those brochures that we had been collecting.

"We're still OK financially, but we're certainly not where we used to be. And I worry about what's ahead and what will happen once we've gone through all of our savings. I know that I shouldn't complain. Andrew could have died. I still have him, and we're still together in our own home. I'm sorry to bother you with all of this. There are so many others who have it so much worse than we do. But I just worry all of the time now. And I'm so tired. What will happen to Andrew if I'm not strong enough to keep this up?"

Beverly only came to my office for several sessions. But during that time, we worked well together and made several important changes. Beverly had been taking good care of Andrew, but not of herself. She was mildly depressed, but thoroughly overwhelmed and exhausted. Her primary-care physician started her on a low-dose antidepressant to help with her ongoing difficulty sleeping. Her brother agreed to come over two evenings a week instead of one. So one evening was devoted to errands and the second was reserved for dinner or a movie out with a friend. We found a local caregivers support group that met during Beverly's lunch break from work. Beverly also started an exercise program at home, began a journal to document her sorrows and her joys, and promised to see her physician regularly to monitor her weight and general health condition.

Lastly, Beverly's worries about finances were understandable, especially in light of the reality that she had felt ill-prepared to take over Andrew's role as the person in their marriage who would make all of the financial decisions. So Beverly reluctantly contacted an accountant friend and asked for help in better understanding her current and possibly future economic situation. The friend was happy to help, and spread the word to their other friends. Before Beverly realized it, other friends started offering their assistance. Friends of Andrew's showed up to mow the lawn or take care of small household repairs. Friends of hers showed up once again to "watch" Andrew so Beverly could go for a walk or just catch her breath. Several couples Beverly and Andrew were friends with started coming over one Friday evening each month, bringing pizza and a rental movie to share with this housebound couple. Beverly and Andrew's friends had wanted to help; they just didn't know what to do, and Beverly had seemed so committed to doing everything herself.

I recently ran into Beverly at a local family caregivers conference. She was thin, but no longer appeared ill. Andrew was still being cared for at home and was doing as well as could be expected. Beverly was still his primary caregiver, although she was now more willing to accept help from family, friends, and outside caretakers as needed. She had maintained the changes we had discussed during our prior sessions. She exercises regularly either at home or at a nearby gym. Her journal has become a good emotional outlet for the inevitable frustrations that occur. The family caregivers support group has proven an invaluable source of camaraderie and shared problem-solving. She feels less isolated, with friends coming and going regularly, whether to help around the house or to join in on the now regular Friday-night ritual.

"Life is quieter now and certainly different, but not all bad," says Beverly. "Our friendships are richer, and my time with Andrew is a treasure that I could have lost. It's a privilege to do what I'm doing, and if the tables were turned, he'd be doing it for me. I just needed to catch my breath and do a better job of balancing everything. Letting people help me was a big part of learning to do this right."

THE PHYSICAL CHALLENGES OF
FAMILY CAREGIVING

Andrew and Beverly's story is an inside look at the challenges and stresses of the family caregiver. The physical burden alone can be overwhelming. Family caregiving can be either a part-time or full-time job. It often involves the night shift. Either way, it is physically demanding.

If you are a spousal caregiver, like Beverly, you may be juggling your own employment situation in addition to taking on some of your ill spouse's household responsibilities, along with the actual caretaking tasks now called for. For the first several months at home, Andrew required assistance to walk to the bathroom. This included several nighttime trips. No wonder Beverly was so exhausted. Luckily, Andrew was not a particularly big man; otherwise Beverly would not have been capable of doing what she did for him.

Also, Andrew's daily care did not involve any complex medical treatments, but that is not the case for all family caregivers. Sometimes, family caregiving also includes the uncomfortable challenges of having to learn how to administer multiple medicines or other intimidating treatments to your loved one. And what if there are also children in the home who are still in need of parenting? Or if you are the family caregiver for an aging, ailing parent but still have your own family to attend to? These are common scenarios for many of us these days.

FINANCIAL STRESSES

Many households are struggling to meet the financial challenges connected with caring at home for a loved one. This "labor of love" does not come cheaply. Family caregiving arrangements often involve employment changes like those made by Andrew and Beverly. Additionally outside caretakers, rehab services such as physical or occupational therapy, or necessary ongoing medical treatments all represent costly additions to a potentially constricted family budget.

CAREGIVER WELL-BEING

Understandably, many family caregivers wind up in a situation similar to Beverly's. They are so busy meeting their loved one's needs and everybody else's needs that they neglect their own well-being. The ill spouse or parent is taken to all of his or her doctors' visits, but the caregiver's health care is often dismissed as too time-consuming or too cumbersome to arrange. Beverly's weight loss appears to have been a manifestation of her exhaustion and caregiver stress, but it could have been an early sign of an unrelated health issue. It was important during our brief work together to help Beverly see that she could only take good care of Andrew if she also took good care of her own physical health and emotional well-being.

CAREGIVER GRIEF

But family caregiving is not just about stress; it is about a special kind of grief. How do you grieve for someone who is still there? How do you resolve the complex feelings that are evoked when your spouse or parent starts to play the role of a demanding child? If your loved one, be they parent, or spouse, adult sibling or aged aunt, has an illness such as Alzheimer's disease, then you may well need to grieve for the personhood that has been lost even as the body stays behind. You may have to learn how to love and care for someone who has sadly become unlovable and may not even remember who you are. Many caregivers will carry on their daily burdens, seeking the sense of privilege that Beverly alluded to. But they will need to find this source of inner gratification without the benefit of appreciation from their ill or disabled loved one.

FAMILY CHALLENGES

Because of all of these issues, family caregiving is truly an honorable calling, but it is not an easy one, and it is probably not the right choice for every family. Sometimes family caregiving is a reasonable short-term solution, but not a realistic long-term one. Some family relationships will be strengthened by this arrangement, but others will be unhealthily strained.

I have several friends who have wound up needing to make difficult decisions regarding caretaking arrangements for their aged parents. In several instances, concurrent career and family constraints made full-time in-home family caregiving an unworkable option. In others, changes similar to those made by Andrew and Beverly, along with family and outside support, made keeping a loved one at home a reasonable alternative.

Several friends have also struggled with caretaking issues surrounding a parent with whom they have never had a happy relationship. One such acquaintance was able to transcend old hurts and resentments, finding a special kind of grace in doing so. My other friend found herself only becoming more bitter and resentful as she struggled to please her critical, rejecting parent. This friend, reluctantly but perhaps wisely, sought additional outside assistance in the forms of personal counseling and supplemental outside caretakers, to both preserve her own emotional health and to buffer her relationship with her hard-to-please parent.

SUGGESTIONS AND WARNING SIGNS

If you are a family caregiver, please try to be realistic about what you can and cannot do. Ask for and accept help. Consider a caregivers support group. Many local hospitals, churches and/or community centers sponsor such organizations. It helps all of us to know that we are not alone and that others understand and appreciate what we are going through.

Simple things such as eating right, getting some exercise, and getting enough sleep are especially important for anyone who is taking on the many stresses and frustrations of caring for an ill or disabled loved one. Maintaining some regular outside social contact with friends or family members is also crucial to any family caregiver's emotional health. Social isolation is a depleting and demoralizing state of affairs. Despite the sometimes-cumbersome logistics involved, even several hours of social contact can reduce caregiver stress significantly. Similarly, finding an acceptable and nonjudgmental outlet for the many mixed emotions associated with a loved one's ongoing care is also important. Family caregiving is hard enough without carrying around a lot of unnecessary guilt or built-up frustration.

Be kind to yourself; you deserve it.

Despite using all of the previously mentioned strategies, some family caregivers will reach the point of total exhaustion. Some will become depressed, anxious, irritable, or angry all of the time. Others will start to experience weight loss or some other potential sign of ill health. Many will struggle with insomnia. Some will experience stress-ridden urges to either overeat or overindulge in alcohol. All of these warning signs should be taken seriously and attended to. Start with going to see your regular physician for a checkup. You might also consider several sessions of individual counseling to give you some perspective on what may have become an overwhelming situation.

It is important for family caregivers to remember that they can only take good care of their loved one as long as they also take good care of themselves.

PART FOUR

Lessons in Coping for Patients, Families, and Good Friends

Chapter Fourteen

SURVIVORS

Although the world is full of suffering,
it is full also of the overcoming of it.

—Helen Keller

MR. EASYGOING

Tom and I met in the spring of 2009. He was not a patient of
mine, but he was the friend of a colleague of mine. Tom had
heard about the book that I was writing, and he was willing to
share his story in the hopes that it would be helpful to others
dealing with similar circumstances. My colleague had recommended Tom to me because of his markedly optimistic and
upbeat approach to living with cancer. "Tom is just one of those
people that makes you smile," I was told. And it is true.

Tom is a sixty-seven-year-old gentleman with a ready smile
that reaches his eyes. His speaking voice exudes good cheer
and friendliness. He has a keen sense of humor and a good singing voice. Tom would be the first to tell you that he is blessed in
many ways. He and his wife of forty-nine years have six children and eleven grandchildren, all of whom live nearby and
get together frequently. Tom is retired now, but was once a
successful businessman.

At the time of our initial meeting, Tom was feeling pretty good. He and his wife hoped to do some more traveling, but meanwhile he was enjoying playing golf, singing in his church choir, and having Sunday dinners with his children and grandchildren. Listening to Tom's lighthearted laugh, you would never know that he was a recent cancer survivor.

In August 2007, Tom and his wife were ready to leave on a long-awaited trip to Nova Scotia. But before they left, Tom visited his primary-care physician to get some medication for the annoying "sinus headaches" he had been experiencing for several weeks. That seemingly straightforward doctor's visit led to a series of tests and the discovery of a brain tumor. This led to more tests and the diagnosis of lymphoma. Needless to say, the Nova Scotia trip was canceled. A year of chemotherapy treatments took its place.

Tom is quick to reassure me that he has had it much easier than many of his friends who have had cancer. He does acknowledge that two-thirds of the way through a very aggressive chemotherapy course, he "crashed." This was a challenging time for Tom. He was quite ill and very weak. He tells me that the hard part was not the physical discomfort as much as losing his independence. Having his wife push his wheelchair for him was a difficult psychological pill to swallow.

But Tom doesn't think that he ever got depressed during his ordeal, and he never lost hope. He did, however, feel bad about the worry that his illness was causing his wife and his children. He attributes this emotional resilience to a "pretty good outlook on life," along with his tendency to be patient and easygoing, as well as a large support network of family and friends.

At the time of our first meeting, Tom was getting imaging studies every four months to watch for any signs of a recurrence. Multiple scans had thus far found him cancer-free. Reportedly, he doesn't spend a lot of time worrying about his cancer coming back, but he is trying to take better care of himself in general. I asked Tom for any advice he might want to give to others dealing with a serious illness. He quickly responded, "Find doctors that you can trust and then listen to them; try to keep a positive attitude; and lean on those who want to help you."

I recently reconnected with Tom by phone. In August 2009, a routine scan revealed that his cancer had returned. It had been two years since his original diagnosis. Tom is back in active treatment and expects another six to nine months of chemotherapy. He reports being tired again, but otherwise doing well.

His voice still sounds rich, strong, and upbeat. He joked with me about a doctor's recent comment that the tumor was in a "nonessential" part of his brain. "Nonessential for what?" he laughingly asked me. On a more serious note, Tom did acknowledge being both surprised and disappointed with the news of this recent recurrence. But he was quick to add, "You know how it is; you just pick yourself up and do what you have to and hope for the best."

ROUND TWO

Mary has been a professional nurse for more than thirty years. She has held different positions over time, but currently teaches at a university-based school of nursing. She is an attractive, animated, and well-spoken woman. Mary is also mother of three, married to her high school sweetheart, and a two-time cancer survivor.

Round one started five years ago. Mary found a small lump in her left breast. She wasn't overwhelmingly alarmed at the time. Her family had no history of breast cancer, and she was otherwise feeling quite well. However, further testing confirmed that she did indeed have breast cancer.

After consulting with both a surgeon and oncologist, Mary's treatment plan was eventually decided upon. She would have a partial mastectomy followed by thirty-three radiation treatments. Although her diagnosis was made the week before Thanksgiving, the treatment plan was not solidified until shortly before Christmas, so Mary and her husband chose to wait until after the holidays to tell their children and their families this unexpected diagnostic news.

Mary remembers being surprised and initially overwhelmed with this unanticipated turn of events in her life. But mostly, she remembers that this first cancer came at an especially inconvenient time. Her middle child was in the midst of a significant personal crisis, and Mary felt her cancer was "just in the way." So that winter, Mary had her first surgery, followed by radiation treatments until mid-April.

Mary describes this first experience with cancer treatment as fatiguing but not otherwise particularly difficult. She took only two days off for her surgery and scheduled each of her radiation treatments at the end of a workday in order to limit any disruption of her work life. She was told that she had a 95 percent survival rate post-treatment, so there was every reason to be optimistic.

For the next several years, Mary's life was almost back to normal. Her middle child's personal crisis was gradually resolving and she herself was no longer an active cancer patient. But she was a recent cancer survivor, so that meant several years of follow-up care. For the first two years, she was scanned for any new signs of cancer every three months. Then it was every six months, for the next two years. Each time, she held her breath, hoped for the best, and then breathed a huge sigh of relief when all was well.

And then, one year ago, an annual mammogram revealed another tumor. The now-familiar diagnostics were once again completed and unfortunately confirmed that Mary's cancer was back. This news was harder to take. This news was harder to share with her spouse, her children, and their extended family members. Mary reports that it was especially difficult to share this news of a cancer recurrence with her elderly parents. "They don't need this type of worry and stress at this point in their lives. I'm supposed to be here to take care of them." So Mary was angrier this time. Round two was more than an inconvenience. It upset and frightened her family, and it disrupted her plans to complete her doctoral education.

The treatment course for this second cancer experience was also more difficult. This time Mary would need a complete mastectomy and chemotherapy. This time, she would also need to make a decision about reconstructive surgery. Chemo came first and then surgery. Mary's course of chemotherapy was more difficult to tolerate than her earlier course of radiation treatments. Over the next several months, she would be hospitalized twice for infections. She would spend a month at home on intravenous antibiotics. She would feel exhausted and she lost her lovely hair. Much to her frustration and dismay, Mary discovered that her insurance company would not cover the cost of a wig. They would, however, cover the cost of several sessions of psychotherapy to help her deal with her distress about her cancer and her hair loss. Mary chose to fight that battle, and eventually was reimbursed for her wig. But she still fumes about the needless frustration she experienced over this and other issues with the system.

Mary's ten-hour surgery took place in May 2009. She then spent a week in the hospital and two and a half months at home recuperating. Mary is now back at work full-time, is still receiving some hormonal treatments, and has yet to schedule the second round of her reconstructive surgery. But after that, she hopes that "this chapter of my life will be over with."

Mary remains optimistic about her future, although she is thoroughly aware that her second round of breast cancer increases her risk for future cancers. She attributes her positive attitude and strong coping style to "great support, great doctors, and great faith. I prayed a lot. I just didn't feel finished with the things that I have to do on earth, so I just had to get through this."

In the depth of winter, I finally learned that within me there lay an invincible summer.

—ALBERT CAMUS

However, Mary does acknowledge that as a second-time cancer survivor, she still struggles to adjust to her altered body image and still works very hard to keep any new symptoms in perspective. "It's easy to start to fret with every new ache and pain. After all, it's happened twice, so surely it can happen again. But I'm learning to live with that uncertainty every day. Every day is a new challenge, but I just choose to be hopeful, get up, and go on with my day."

Mary's advice for others dealing with a cancer diagnosis is to ask lots of questions and be sure to bring someone with you to your appointments. "Especially early on, you're just so overwhelmed. You can't process it all. Even as a knowledgeable health-care provider, I needed my husband to help me remember and translate what had been said during office visits." Mary made the decision to seek out physicians who specialized in her particular form of cancer. She found it reassuring to work with the experts in the field. She also found it helpful, especially the second time, to tell more people and accept the help they offered. Mary didn't make it to a support group per se, but she knows several other women at the university who are cancer survivors, so they meet and share stories often. "Talking about it helps, especially with people who really understand what you're going through."

Lastly, Mary comments that her cancer experiences and survivorship have changed her perspective. "I used to be pretty anal-retentive; everything needed to be just so. But I've learned that plans can go out the window in a heartbeat. So I focus on the big things and don't let life's little details get me down. I also appreciate my good friends and family members very intensely right now. I don't want to lose that feeling." Like Tom, Mary also comments on how very lucky she is. "I've had great support, and I am so fortunate that we found that first cancer early. Others aren't as lucky as I've been."

CANCER SURVIVORS

Having a life-threatening illness changes people. In fact, any face-to-face confrontation with possible extinction, whether via a serious illness, a near-miss accident, or a natural disaster is a powerful existential blow. Once you have had a near-death experience, you can't kid yourself that you are invulnerable or that your inevitable death is comfortably and predictably years away. Almost dying is a dramatic reminder that there are no guarantees in this life. What is here one moment, can be forever gone the next.

Surviving an illness such as cancer can be even more complicated. Thanks to major advances in cancer treatment, many individuals diagnosed with a potentially life-threatening cancer will be fortunate enough to spend years and years living as cancer survivors. This is good news, but it brings new psychological challenges to the forefront.

Many cancer survivors will have to cope with not only an uncomfortably heightened sense of personal mortality, but also the multiple uncertainties now associated with cancer survivorship: Will my original cancer recur? Am I now at risk for another, second cancer? What about the long-term, so-called late effects of my original cancer treatment? Living with uncertainty short-term is hard enough, but how do you cope with uncertainty for years and years?

Some of my cancer survivor clients approach these challenges in a manner similar to what Tom and Mary have described for us. They are truly humbled and appreciative of their good fortune. They have survived a very real threat to their lives, and they are grateful. They are committed to taking good care of their now precious health and enjoying the gifts that come with each new day. They choose not to overly focus on the uncertainties of their future. They will readily go to see their physicians if they are feeling unwell, but otherwise they will go about their days under the hopeful assumption that they are healthy and all is well.

But others struggle to keep the uncertainties and fears of survivorship at bay. Every new pain, no matter how minor, is an anxiety-provoking reminder that the cancer may have come back. This ongoing and vigilant scanning for the next round of bad news corrupts the joy of each new day. It is very sad to see someone who had been successfully treated for a life-threatening disease such as cancer spend his or her remaining days living in fear of what may or may not ever occur.

Many survivors live somewhere in between take-one-day-at-a-time gratitude and incessant worry. But anyone who is too anxiety-ridden to go on with his or her life in a productive and meaningful way should consider either individual or group support. It is possible to live with uncertainty. You just have to find a place for it.

Anyone who has survived a life-threatening illness deserves to celebrate life. Some survivors will do so naturally, but others will be traumatized by these experiences and will need additional support.

Fortunately within the field of oncology, there is a growing awareness that psychological services are needed to assist some individuals in coping with the uncertainties of disease survivorship. The challenging psychological journey of the cancer survivor is finally being recognized and supported. The goal of successful cancer survivorship is not denial of the uncertainty and risks that still exist. Instead, the goal is putting that uncertainty in perspective and going on with one's life. It is not possible to totally forget that you had cancer and may have it again, but it is possible to choose to live each new day in celebration of the gift at hand. On a positive note, despite the obstacles encountered, most cancer survivors do describe a life well worth living.

SURVIVORS OF A DIFFERENT SORT

I recently met with three women friends who are also widows. I asked each of them for thoughts about their strategies for coping with the loss of a spouse and surviving the challenges of widowhood. Interestingly, their comments were very similar, despite significant differences in their personalities and the circumstances under which they became widows.

My friend Susan has been widowed for twelve years. Her husband died after a long illness. She was widowed after a thirty-year marriage. Susan admits that she struggled initially, in part because she failed to accept the support offered by friends. I was one of those friends, and I remember trying to reach out, but being rebuffed. Susan shares, "I didn't want to feel vulnerable or weak, so I mistakenly tried to handle my grief and the transition to widowhood alone." We are close friends once again, but it took a while for our relationship to relearn how to share and support each other. Susan now readily admits, "Accepting help from others can be a sign of strength, not weakness."

Jane's husband also died after a prolonged illness, but she is a new widow. Cal died only eighteen months ago. Jane has two school-age children to parent single-handedly now, but luckily she also has a large extended family network living nearby. Jane shared that getting through all those firsts of the initial year was as difficult as she had expected it to be. She found that anticipating and planning ahead helped significantly. So, for example, she gave careful thought as to how to spend the first family Christmas without Cal. Despite the advice of several well-intentioned acquaintances, Jane chose not to travel to a new and different location. She chose to celebrate the holiday in her and Cal's family home but invited all of the nearby relatives, including her in-laws. This may not have been the right answer for every widow, but it was the right thing for Jane and her children.

Jane told me, "Leaning on others through the tough times

has helped me immensely. I know that if I falter, I will have friends or family that will be there to pick me up and set me on my feet again." Jane added, "Spending our first holiday season surrounded by loving and supportive relatives was exactly what I and the kids needed, but in order to figure that out, I had to learn to trust my own inner voice. I also had to learn that it was OK for me to tell my friends and relatives what I needed from them."

Maggie is a young widow. She lost her husband of only six years, suddenly. Maggie spoke to the particular challenges of being a young widow because it is so much harder to find women her own age in a similar circumstance. Maggie has no children and travels frequently for her job with a local consulting firm. Maggie used an online support service for widows to locate other young widows in her age group.

According to Maggie, "The most important step that I've taken to survive as a widow has been to find other widows. I've also had to learn to trust my own judgment as to what is best for me right now. For example, most of my old friends told me that I should wait before emptying out Pete's bedroom closet. But my new widow friends just told me to do whatever felt right for me—and I did. I needed to get Pete's things out of the bedroom so that I could sleep." Maggie added, "I'm learning that there is no formula to surviving as a widow; we each have to find our own way."

GOOD ADVICE

Tom, Mary, Susan, Jane, and Maggie are all survivors of life-altering events. Each has demonstrated grace and courage as they have learned to cope with the anxieties and stresses of the unwanted and unexpected new lives that they are now living.

Despite their very different stories, they seem to agree when it comes to the advice that they have for the rest of us. There are no simple formulas or straightforward, one-size-fits-all rules for surviving either a serious illness or the loss of a loved one. Being a cancer survivor or a widow involves a complex series of transitions and adjustments. Each person will need to find his or her own way. But according to these survivors, there is one golden rule of survivorship that we can all count on:

During the hard times, we should each learn to reach out and accept the support of others.

Chapter Fifteen

GOOD
THOUGHTS

An optimist sees an opportunity in every calamity.
A pessimist sees a calamity in every opportunity.

—WINSTON CHURCHILL

HALF FULL OR HALF EMPTY?

What does it mean to be either an optimist or a pessimist? And why does it matter? Usually optimism is defined as a tendency to look for or expect favorable outcomes. So-called optimists are often noticeably upbeat and fun to be with. Conversely, pessimism is the tendency to anticipate unfavorable outcomes. This latter pattern understandably leads to more negative, dispirited demeanors.

But optimism and pessimism as they have been described above are not all-or-nothing states. They represent opposite poles on a personality continuum. Most people live somewhere in the middle of these two polarities. However, many of us tend to consistently lean in one direction or the other. So stop and think for a minute. Do you consider yourself generally optimistic or pessimistic? How would your family members or good friends describe you? Has your predilection toward optimism or pessimism changed over the years? If so, do you know why?

Most of us have had the opportunity while watching our local news or weather channel on television to witness a family reacting to the devastation of a recent fire, flood, or hurricane. The television camera pans the rubble that was once a home, and then focuses on the dazed victims of the so-called natural disaster.

Sometimes the traumatized family will tearfully speak of everything that has been lost—not just their home but also all of the irreplaceable possessions within that home. But other individuals will share how blessed they feel to have survived unharmed, despite the visible leveling of the family residence just behind them. Both viewpoints are true. The proverbial cup is simultaneously half empty and half full. But the person who is able to see the cup as half full is usually better positioned to deal with adversity.

In May 2008, Dr. Randy Pausch attended Carnegie Mellon's commencement exercise as an invited guest speaker. Randy was quite ill at this point in time, but the opportunity to visit his beloved campus one more time was compelling. When the commencement ceremony was completed, Randy, dressed formally in his academic robes, started to process out of the arena. Reportedly, the entire audience, comprised of colleagues, the student body, new graduates, and their families, all stood up and cheered as Dr. Pausch exited for one last time.

Randy and his wife, Jai, came to my office the next day for a counseling session. Randy was beaming as he described the prior day's heartwarming ovation after graduation. According to Randy, at that moment the sun shone brightly and the air was filled with love, support, and positive energy. With tears in his eyes, Randy declared, "I am the luckiest man alive." And he meant it. Randy Pausch died from pancreatic cancer only two short months later. Randy was a born optimist.

A relative of mine was recently diagnosed with a chronic and potentially disabling illness at a relatively young age. This special man has a young family with two school-age children and thus many years of child rearing still ahead. His illness's rate of progression is unclear at this point in time, but eventually it may be both life-limiting and life-altering.

And yet in response to this clearly unwelcome deviation in an otherwise hopeful-looking midlife script, my family member has repeatedly reminded the rest of our family how very fortunate he is to have so much time to plan and prepare for whatever will ultimately be his fate. He will hopefully have time to actively parent his children until they are grown or at least almost grown. He will have time to financially prepare so that his young wife will be cared for when he can no longer provide for her.

"After all, think about all of the young or middle-aged husbands and fathers who are taken suddenly through the tragic misfortune of a war or a car accident," he says. Reluctantly, my good-hearted relative will admit that he is somewhat disappointed that his longstanding fantasy of a golden retirement, spending many leisure hours on the golf course, is probably no longer very realistic. However, he is quick to wryly comment, "Luckily I was never really any good at golf anyway." This, too, is optimism and positive coping.

This kind of optimism is more than the inclination to anticipate favorable outcomes. It is also the capacity to be aware of the positives that still exist despite coexisting negatives. It is the ability to remember that the cup can be both half full *and* half empty. It is the ability to find comfort in the things that you still have, despite all that you have lost or will be losing. This way of viewing life is an amazing gift if you come by it naturally, but if you don't, it is well worth cultivating.

This conceptualization of optimism is what we might also refer to as "a positive attitude." This is not denial; it is simply the process by which we can choose to not allow present or anticipated negative events to negate all that is good in our lives. A positive attitude also requires the ability to see the silver lining of possibility in the midst of the dark clouds of unwelcome realities.

Some of us are born optimists, but most are not. And it is certainly easier to have a positive attitude when all is well and much more challenging to do so when all is not well. One might assume that having a positive attitude probably contributes to an individual's capacity to relax and enjoy life a bit more. But clearly, possessing a positive attitude can be a powerful asset during the more painful times in our lives.

OBSTACLE OR OPPORTUNITY?

Serious illness, dying, grief, the loss of a family home, and the transition to widowhood can all be described as life crises. Theoretically, a crisis can be anything that shakes our daily equilibrium to the core. These are the times in life when it feels like the sky has fallen and you no longer know where you are or even *who* you are. Some crises are individual in nature. Others happen to families. And then there are national crises, such as September 11, 2001.

From a psychological perspective, how each of us reacts to a crisis situation will depend in part on how we subjectively define or perceive the experience. Is this unwanted situation a challenging opportunity or an immobilizing obstacle? Are we each thinking of ourselves as the unluckiest person in the world or are we going through a difficult time but still so much more fortunate than so many others? Our individual inclination toward optimism or pessimism will help determine how we choose to define our new reality.

Being told that you have a life-threatening illness can be both an individual and a family crisis of significant proportions. It is a sad and scary place to be. It is also an experience that tends to put all others into perspective. Issues and concerns that once loomed so large may become quite trivial. Health, time, and relationships become so much more important as other things become less so. Serious illness is also an opportunity to truly appreciate and use the remaining time well. Anyone who has lost a loved one suddenly and unexpectedly will readily attest to the value of that particular opportunity.

Having a loved one with a serious illness tends to have a similar effect. It is heartbreaking and yet can also be perspective-enhancing. Time together is precious and no longer taken for granted, despite the grief that waits around the corner of each new day. Remember that proverbial cup; it truly can be both half empty and half full at the same time. Doors are closing, but perhaps windows are opening.

If a crisis immobilizes and demoralizes us, it will limit our innate ability to cope and solve problems. This defeat may well diminish our resilience to future hardships. The opposite is also true. If we are somehow able to proactively move through a crisis period, we may achieve a sense of personal mastery and a strengthened coping repertoire that will serve us well in the future. You have only to listen to the pride in a new widow's voice after she has balanced a checkbook for the first time or when she looks back after the first year without her mate and realizes that she and the children are actually doing well, in order to appreciate that overcoming these hurdles is ego-strengthening.

Viewing a crisis as a challenge gives us room to problem-solve. Viewing the same crisis as an overwhelming obstacle creates a sense of helpless victimhood.

GOOD THOUGHTS

So how do we get ourselves to think about a serious crisis such as a life-threatening illness or the loss of a loved one as a heart-breaking challenge to be dealt with versus a doomsday script? Cognitive therapists teach their clients that their moods or feelings are often determined by their thoughts. In other words, when we are feeling depressed or anxious, most of us spend a good deal of time thinking pretty negative thoughts. We tend to focus on worst-case scenarios along with the irrational belief that we will definitely not be able to handle whatever bad stuff is coming our way. And we often add to this pattern of doomful prophecy and lack of confidence a hurtful measure of anticipatory worry that no matter what happens, things will only get worse.

I am an old man, who has known many problems. Most of which have never happened.

—MARK TWAIN

As Twain's humorous but salient quotation suggests, there is potential for a great deal of unnecessary emotional wear and tear when we immerse ourselves in the world of negative thinking. The good news is that with some conscious effort and practice, many people can successfully lessen their tendency toward catastrophic or pessimistic thinking.

Life comes with no guarantees. Really bad things can happen to very nice people. But while we cannot totally control what happens to us, we can choose to exert a major effort toward reacting to unwanted hardships in a positive, constructive fashion. We cannot always change a situation, but we can control our attitude toward that situation and our reaction to it. We can choose to make the best of a difficult circumstance. We can choose to solve problems one by one. We can choose to help ourselves and support our loved ones as best we can. We can choose to not make things worse by immersing ourselves in self-pity or self-defeat. We all may find ourselves visiting the land of despair when facing challenging circumstances, but we should make a determined effort not to stay there too long.

> *We cannot change the cards we are dealt, just how we play the hand.*
>
> —RANDY PAUSCH

We can choose to try to push away our immobilizing and defeatist initial reactions or negative thoughts in order to free our energies for the problem-solving that lies ahead. Repeatedly telling yourself, "I can't do this" or "I'll never get through this" or "I'm never going to be happy again" will only serve to make you hurt even more and is most likely neither accurate nor predictive.

Being seriously ill or newly bereaved involves so very many transitions, new challenges, and big or small problems to be solved. Thinking these self-defeating and usually inaccurate (or at least exaggerated) negative thoughts doesn't leave you with the energy and goal-directed sense of purpose that you will need in order to approach these transitions and problems one small step at a time.

Many people adopt personal mantras, such as negative thoughts being "not helpful right now" or "I'm not there yet" or "I'm going to take one day at a time right now" so they can push away self-defeating or anxiety-provoking thoughts. Other possibly helpful mantras include "I *can* do this" or "Eventually, I will get where I need to go" or "I am doing the best that I can right now and that will have to be good enough."

Hint: if what you are thinking about your crisis situation helps you to feel more hopeful or capable and helps you to get through another difficult day, then it's probably a good thing. However, if your thoughts only serve to discourage you and make you even more overwhelmed than you already are, then it might be time to question their usefulness and perhaps seek ways to either more effectively encourage yourself or give yourself permission to get some extra outside help until you're feeling better.

Bad times are hard enough without us making it harder on ourselves. We each need to learn how to support and comfort ourselves. We each need to learn how to be our own cheerleaders, when the game of life is not going in our favor. We all deserve comfort, support, and encouragement. It's nice to get it from others. But we also need to learn how to give it to ourselves.

Besides positive thinking and proactive coping, another trait that I have observed in many of my more optimistic clients is the capacity to truly appreciate the joy of the moment. These individuals do not lose their ability to truly relish the small pleasures of life, regardless of whatever adverse circumstance they are confronting. Sadness and suffering have not robbed them of their ability to remain attuned to the big and small gifts of each new day.

This is a very here-and-now, focused attitude. It requires

that at least some of the time you give yourself permission to just be, instead of always thinking about where you have been or where you are going. This focused appreciation of the moment is an opportunity that is easily missed and yet it so enhances our capacity to live the gift of life fully.

When is the last time that you allowed yourself the time to truly savor a good cup of coffee instead of just gulping it down as you rush out the door? When is the last time that you gave yourself permission to spend an hour at the park, watching children or puppies play, just because it's nice to witness such simple innocence? When is the last time you sang or laughed out loud? What about taking time to appreciate how wonderful a cool breeze feels on a hot, humid day or, conversely, what a pleasure it is to snuggle under a soft comforter on a cold, wintry day? What big or small things did you appreciate about your day today? What about yesterday?

I have seen a seriously ill man tear up at the sight of a striking sunset, simply because he was so very touched by the loveliness in his world. I have seen a woman exhausted and sick to her stomach after yet another round of chemo stop and smile at a giggling baby, even as she struggled back into her wheelchair. We all need to remember to take the time to appreciate simple pleasures and to cultivate our ability to do so, regardless of whether we are simply hurried or coping with a life crisis.

GRATITUDE

Gratitude is appreciation with a thank-you attached. Gratitude is punctuated by a constant awareness that regardless of your particular circumstance, there will be others who are struggling even more. Gratitude is the opposite of self-pity. Gratitude implies that

I choose to remain grateful for what I have despite whatever I don't have. Gratitude does not invite bitterness or envy to the table.

I am touched and humbled when my seriously ill patients tell me how fortunate they are compared to others, despite their obvious personal suffering. These individuals remain genuinely grateful that their children or grandchildren are well, or grateful that they will have enough time to put their affairs in order. And of course, many of my patients are so very grateful for all of the love and support that they receive from their family and friends. This ability to put one's own suffering into perspective and to remain appreciative of the good things in one's life despite very real hardships is another key ingredient in maintaining a positive attitude during difficult times.

If the only prayer that you ever say in your entire life is thank you, it will be enough.

—Meister Eckhart

KEY INGREDIENTS

This chapter has been about choosing to approach a difficult situation with a positive attitude. The important word here is "choosing." It may not feel like it at the time, but in spite of the many things that you lose control over during a serious illness or grief experience, there are still other aspects of your life and coping style that remain within your control.

One of these choices is trying to adopt a more optimistic and positive attitude. Some individuals respond automatically to adversity with grace, optimism, and proactive problem-solving. But others will have to work at it. I truly believe that cultivating your capacity for optimism and proactive problem-solving is worth the effort. Similarly, I genuinely believe that learning to do an even better job of comforting and encouraging yourself is not only a necessary survival skill for difficult times, it is also something that we all deserve to give ourselves.

There is nothing weak or abnormal about initially responding to a life crisis in an overwhelmed and discouraged manner. But the only way through—is through. So sooner or later we each need to find a way to put one foot in front of the other, survive, and hopefully cope constructively. For those readers who are fortunate enough to not be in a life crisis at this point in time, it might still be worthwhile to give some thought as to how you might enhance your capacity to sustain a positive attitude before the inevitable traumas of serious illness, death, or grief touch your life or the lives of those you care about.

As a review, the overlapping but key ingredients to this recipe for "learned optimism" include:

1. Cultivate your capacity to be aware of the positives in your life, despite any coexisting negatives.
2. Choose to see adversity as a challenge or an opportunity instead of a threat or an immobilizing obstacle.
3. Take time to be in the present instead of the past or future, and give yourself permission to appreciate the small pleasures of the moment.
4. Remember that whatever difficulties you encounter, there will be others whose struggles are greater. This will help you keep perspective.
5. On a daily basis, remind yourself to be not only aware of but also grateful for what you have instead of dwelling on what you do not have.

Chapter Sixteen

BEARING
WITNESS

Can I see another's woe,
And not be in sorrow, too?
Can I see another's grief,
And not seek for kind relief?

—WILLIAM BLAKE

A GOOD LISTENER

There is a remarkable difference between being asked how you are by someone who keeps on walking by versus being asked the exact same question by someone who actually stops, pauses, looks at you, and patiently waits for your response. In the latter circumstance, this acquaintance has conveyed without any additional words that he or she truly cares about you and how you are feeling that day. Listening is a skill. You have probably already noticed that some people are better listeners than others.

What makes a good listener? Or perhaps the converse question is more helpful. What makes a bad listener? Think about it. We could generate a list of helpful behavioral hints such as good eye contact and attentive postures. But it may be more meaningful to suggest that a good listener is someone who makes you feel heard, cared about, and understood.

> *A good listener is anyone who seems to genuinely*
> *want to hear what you have to say.*

Good listening is qualitatively different from the passive stance of paying partial attention that is part and parcel of many everyday conversations. Good listening is active and empathetic. It takes energy to actively listen. However, good listening does not require sophisticated communication skills; it doesn't even require agreeing with what the other person is saying. Good listening simply takes a little extra time. Having a good listener in your life is a true blessing.

SOCIAL ISOLATION

Being seriously ill is essentially an isolating experience. At the most basic level, you are often confined to bed while everybody else gets to move around and do the usual everyday things. If you are seriously ill but living at home, you will spend much of your day resting in your sickbed while listening to the sounds of life going on without you, elsewhere in the family home. If you are quite ill and spending time in a hospital, you will experience a different kind of isolation from your loved ones and what was once your daily family life. Even more powerfully, other lives will go on, whereas yours may or may not. Others can care about you, even love you, but they cannot feel your pain or your fear. They may certainly experience their own pain and suffering, but it will not take yours away.

Being the family member of a dying loved one can also be a very lonely and overwhelming experience. Most people, understandably, feel ill-equipped for this sad caretaking responsibility. Other daily tasks usually do not stop when one is caring for an ill loved one. Young children still need their mother's attention even if she is also caring for their ailing father. Adult children who have assumed responsibility for an aging and ill parent may still have their own households, including a spouse and possibly adolescents, to attend to. These are exhausting times with little opportunity for leisure activity or needed social support. Even when they would truly appreciate the support or social companionship of others, most caretakers are routinely too overwhelmed and exhausted to initiate any social contact. Even asking for much-needed help can seem too cumbersome a task to accomplish.

Social isolation and loneliness are demoralizing human conditions. Some of us may crave attention more than others, but none of us thrive when left totally alone. Serious illness, caregiving, and grieving are essentially lonely journeys, but they can be made less so. If you are the relative or friend of someone who is seriously ill, grieving, or taking care of a loved one, there are things that you can say and do to provide meaningful support during these difficult times.

This chapter is about the power of just listening and being available. Sometimes there are no magic words. But even if we cannot make the situation better, we can make it less lonely. Bearing witness to someone else's suffering instead of turning away or avoiding is a healing gesture unto itself. It is also a brave and generous thing to do.

Friends and family members of the seriously ill or recently bereaved should understand that simply being present and available is an act of great courage and a gift of great comfort.

SOCIAL AVOIDANCE

Many people shy away from uncomfortable social situations with an ill or newly bereaved acquaintance or friend simply

because they don't know what to say. These well-meaning acquaintances and friends want to be helpful, but fear being hurtful. They don't want to say the wrong thing. They also feel
unprepared to cope with any unexpected emotional outbursts
on the part of their sick or grieving friend. Perhaps some of these
friends are also uncomfortably aware of the relief that they are
experiencing that the tragedy that has struck their friend's
home luckily did not befall theirs instead. So they avoid social
contact or they simply don't say anything about the potentially
sad topic at hand.

Unfortunately, this awkward avoidance leaves the ill or bereaved friend feeling even more isolated and uncared for. Their
sick or grief-stricken friend is asking themselves, "Do people not
know, or do they just not care?" Sadly, this lack of preparedness
and the resulting avoidance can manifest itself among family
members as well as friends and coworkers.

WHAT TO SAY AND WHAT NOT TO SAY

When in doubt, keep it simple: "I'm so sorry that you're going
through this." No one who is coping with a life-threatening illness or the recent loss of a loved one expects the rest of us to have
the answer to his or her plight. But we all deserve to feel cared
about during times of great sadness and loss. You are simply ex-
pressing your caring, concern, and compassion. And you should
not underestimate the power and importance of doing so.

On the other hand, it is usually best to avoid the temptation
to overly identify with your struggling friend or to make pre-
mature attempts to cheer them up. The phrase "I know how
you feel" is usually not a helpful one. Remember, each of our
illness or loss experiences is unique and therefore special. Each
of our reactions to these situations is a personal one, so none of

us can truly totally understand what another person is going through. It is far more beneficial to allow a struggling friend to share what he or she chooses of their individual journey and for you to sensitively and caringly listen. The exception to this general rule occurs when individuals who have gone through similar experiences join for mutual support. An example would be a support group for bereaved parents, where each person there has earned membership into that particular group of shared understanding and grief.

Similarly well-intended but poorly timed early efforts to comfort or reassure a hurting companion tend to create a sense of distance rather than the hoped-for consolation. Statements such as "You're so young, I'm sure you'll have other children" (after a miscarriage) or "I'm sure you'll marry again and be quite happy someday" (to console a young widow) inadvertently minimize the pain of acute grief and thus provide no comfort at all. Hopefully these positive predictions will be quite accurate someday, but that does not negate the need to grieve first for what has been lost. Again, be there and listen. If you do, your friends will wind up telling you where they are and what they need from you.

SMALL GESTURES

However, if simply being there and listening is not your strong suit, take heart. There are still small but very practical and meaningful ways to be present and available to those in need. These helpful gestures don't need to be large, but they should be specific. And they should allow the person on the receiving end to say "yes" or "no thank you." The oft-used "Please don't hesitate to call me if you need anything" is well-intentioned but less effective than the following: "I'm on my way to the food store; can I pick up anything for you?" or "I'm taking my own kids to the park this afternoon, would it be convenient for me to stop over and take your kids along too? That way, you can have some time to yourself."

Another helpful strategy is to initiate regular contact with your ill or grieving friend or relative. The nature of your relationship and geographic logistics will determine whether this contact is by phone or in person and whether it is every several days, weekly, or perhaps monthly. This arrangement of ongoing support recognizes that serious illness and bereavement are journeys over time with ups, downs, and changing needs as time passes. This commitment to continued support is also a powerful way to reassure your friend or relative that his or her plight will not be forgotten when the proverbial dust of the unexpected crisis has settled.

Sending a condolence card upon hearing of someone's serious illness or recent loss is another small but kind and meaningful gesture. In these days of Internet communications, perhaps some things are still best handwritten personally. The purpose of a condolence card is simply to let people know that you are sadly aware of their unfortunate circumstance and thinking of them.

Don't be offended, however, if your caring gesture is not immediately acknowledged. Remember that the person on the receiving end of your card and hopefully many other cards is probably somewhat overwhelmed and exhausted. Responding to multiple condolence cards can be its own difficult task for someone who is seriously ill or newly bereaved. So assume that your kind message was heard and received, whether you get a response or not.

Much like the recommended strategy of ongoing social contact already mentioned, another means of accomplishing a similar goal is to send a second personal note several weeks or months after your initial condolence card, simply indicating the person is still in your thoughts. You can add that you hope he or she is finding some comfort and support during a difficult time. If you choose to, you can suggest getting together whenever they are ready, or you can make a specific offer of support that you would be comfortable providing. But the latter is not necessary. Again, the power of this follow-up note is that it lets your friends or relatives know that they, and what they are going through, are not forgotten.

I have had countless beleaguered family caregivers or traumatized new widows comment with tears in their eyes how truly touched they are by these seemingly inconsequential overtures. The very fact that others around them are cognizant of their plight despite their own busy lives touches them deeply and makes a dent in the disheartening loneliness of their days. One new widow likened these healing gestures to small rays of sunshine on an otherwise cloudy day. These touchpoints of human kindness can provide a temporary but welcome burst of reenergizing hopefulness for better days ahead.

BROKENHEARTED

Laura was a charming and lovely woman in her mid-forties. She was soft-spoken, with the tinge of a Southern drawl retained from a childhood spent in the Carolinas. Laura was happily married to a successful lawyer, a truly kind man. They had three daughters who ranged in age from their early to mid-twenties. They had a lovely home in a nice neighborhood and entertained their many long-term friends graciously and often. Laura had a seemingly picture-book-perfect life, until the fateful phone call that every parent dreads changed her world forever.

Laura's youngest daughter, Clare, had been seriously injured in a car accident. Clare and her mother had had a particularly close relationship. They talked on the phone almost every day and cherished each and every moment that they spent together. Clare had recently graduated from college and was engaged to her high school sweetheart. Clare and her mother had recently gone wedding-gown shopping. Tragically, these wedding plans were derailed by an encounter with a drunk driver.

Laura held herself together long enough to drive safely to her daughter's out-of-town hospital bed. After a three-day vigil, she found the strength to agree to the doctors' recommendation to withdraw her daughter's life support. She stayed at her daughter's bedside until all hope and life were gone. And then she came home and fell apart.

Laura's husband brought her to see me. Although in the throes of his own grief, he was concerned and frightened by the intensity of his wife's distress. Laura's pain was palpable. She could not sleep; she was losing weight. She had seemingly aged overnight, becoming a caricature of her former self. She sat in my office with tears streaming silently down her face, rocking back and forth. Her suffering could break your heart.

Laura and I worked together for ten months. I saw her frequently and collaborated often with her primary-care physician. I consulted with colleagues and reread articles about complicated grief reactions. Antidepressant medications helped to stabilize her weight loss and provide some much-needed sleep. Laura dearly loved her husband and her two surviving daughters, but the sudden and senseless death of her beloved youngest child had left her psychologically adrift in a world that no longer made sense. She could not make peace with this loss. She wanted it to go away. She wanted Clare back. Eventually,

Laura returned to most of her daily activities. She could sleep; she could eat. But she still suffered.

That spring, Laura's husband was offered an out-of-town promotion. I located a therapist in their new town, and Laura and I said a tearful good-bye. The following spring, I was in a local department store and someone gently tapped me on my shoulder. It was Laura. She was in town preparing for the wedding of her middle daughter. We hugged and she cried. As I stood there feeling saddened by the pain I had been unable to relieve in this woman about whom I so genuinely cared, she whispered in my ear, "Thank you, you saved my life."

Sometimes, all we can do is care, be present, and
bear witness. And sometimes, that's all we need to do.

EPILOGUE

THIS BOOK IS FOR YOU

My brother has pancreatic cancer. We live in Brazil, so we are too far away to see you. Please keep helping people who are in need. Best regards from Brazil.

I have lost my mother and best friend to cancer. In hindsight, I wish that I had gotten some counseling. Those of us touched by cancer appreciate the help you give to patients and their families. Please take care.

I am a forty-two-year-old man with metastatic lung cancer. I believe that I will not survive this illness. Can you help my wife and me find a therapist like you in our area? Any help you can give would be appreciated.

I am a thirty-five-year-old man with pancreatic cancer. My situation is very similar to Randy's. I, too, have young children. Could you please help me find a therapist who does work like yours, in my area?

My wife was diagnosed with breast cancer last year. She is quite ill. We are both therapists, but don't know of anyone who does therapy with couples facing a serious illness. Can you help?

*My daughter has just been diagnosed with brain cancer, and her
dad and I don't know how to help. We are particularly worried
about her children. We don't know what to tell or not tell
them. Can you recommend a therapist in our area?*

Above are several of the many e-mail messages that I have
received since being acknowledged as a psychotherapist who
deals with issues related to serious medical illnesses or grief.
The messages have come from all over the country and abroad.
These messages have come from people of all ages and many
different backgrounds. But these strangers all share a common
goal: the desire to make the best of a difficult situation. Each of
these individuals is reaching out and asking for help in order to
cope as well as possible with the challenges of a life-threatening
illness. *Lessons in Loss and Living* was written for each of these
Internet correspondents and so many others. This book is my
attempt to provide comfort and counsel, along with support and
practical advice, to people I will probably never meet in my
office. We all deserve help when going through difficult times. For
some, that help will be the support of family and friends; for others, the most effective source of guidance will be a support group,
a book, or a therapist.

But there was a second agenda behind the writing of this
compilation of stories. I have been a psychotherapist for more
than thirty years, and every day I get to meet and work with the
most incredible people. On a daily basis, I continue to be in-
spired by the true courage and resiliency of those who do enter
my office for counseling, whether seeking help with a relationship issue, anxiety, depression, serious illness, or grief. So this
book is also my chance to pay tribute to all of the amazing
people I have had the privilege of working with as they have
faced a life-threatening illness or a major loss. I hope that the

glow of their optimism, grace, courage, and positive coping will light the way for the rest of us.

EXTRA WORDS OF WISDOM AND INSPIRATION

One of the true pleasures of writing this book was the need to constantly find inspirational proverbs, sayings, or quotes to add to the text of each chapter. This literary search became a group endeavor with many of my friends, colleagues, and relatives e-mailing me possible contenders. Not all of their generous suggestions made it into the preceding chapters, so here are some additional words of wisdom and encouragement for your perusal:

> *'Tis better to have loved and lost*
> *Than never to have loved at all.*
>
> —ALFRED TENNYSON

> *Given a choice between grief and nothing,*
> *I'd choose grief.*
>
> —WILLIAM FAULKNER

> *When life gives you a hundred reasons to cry,*
> *Show life that you have a thousand reasons to smile.*
>
> —AUTHOR UNKNOWN

> *Every second that you spend angry or upset is a second of happiness*
> *that you can never get back.*
>
> —AUTHOR UNKNOWN

When one door closes, another opens. But we often look so long and so regretfully upon the closed door, that we do not see the one that has opened for us.

—ALEXANDER GRAHAM BELL

The best kind of friend is the kind you can sit on a porch swing with, never say a word, and then walk away feeling like it was the best conversation you ever had.

—AUTHOR UNKNOWN

The happiest people don't necessarily have the best of everything, they just make the most of everything they have.

—AUTHOR UNKNOWN

Yesterday is history.
Tomorrow is a mystery.
Today is a gift.
That's why it's called the present.

—AUTHOR UNKNOWN

BEST WISHES

A family I had recently worked with sent this kind but hopefully truthful note to me: *"We are so very grateful to you for all that you have done for us. You didn't just help us to get through our ordeal, but you taught us how to find joy and love during it, as well. We can't thank you enough."* I hope that this book serves the same purpose for its readers. Eventually it may not be enough to simply put one foot in front of the other and survive a difficult time. We each need to find a way to live and love, despite the obstacles in our path. And we need to find a way to heal and move on when the time is right.

It shouldn't take a life-threatening illness or a significant loss to awaken us to the preciousness of life and relationships. But sometimes it does. The stories and strategies in *Lessons in Loss and Living* will hopefully serve as poignant reminders that a lifetime is a finite gift. To race through our days, to wish our time away, or to not work at important relationships all might be mistakes that we can't afford to make.

During the writing of this book, my father died, my youngest brother was diagnosed with a life-altering illness, and I was diagnosed with a fortunately benign thyroid tumor. I also celebrated my granddaughter's second birthday and helped my youngest child plan for her upcoming wedding. Life is like that. All of our lives will be filled with some measure of joy and sorrow. Some will be expected; others will not. Some of the joys will be more lasting than others. Some of the sorrows will be more hurtful or seemingly more unfair than others. We all need to learn to cherish and celebrate the joys and prepare ourselves to cope constructively with the challenges that life's sorrows inevitably bring.

Lessons in Loss and Living is not really a book about death, dying, and grief: It is a book about hope, inspiration, and the art of living and loving well. It is certainly meant to guide and encourage those who are facing great adversity. But hopefully it will also inspire the rest of us to live our lives fully, generously, and with great joy.

> *Live well, laugh often, sing or dance whether someone is looking or not, and find someone or something to love.*

Best Wishes,
MICHELE A. REISS, PH.D.

RESOURCES

Helpful Books

The following list is not exhaustive, but it does include books that I have both personally read and found helpful, or those that have been highly recommended by clients when they were coping with a serious illness or loss situation.

BOOKS ON DEATH, DYING, AND GRIEVING

Albom, M. *Tuesdays with Morrie*. New York: Doubleday, 1997.

Becvar, D. S. *In the Presence of Grief*. New York: Guilford Press, 2001.

Berezin, N. *After a Loss in Pregnancy*. New York: Simon & Schuster, 1982.

Bramblett, J. *When Good-bye Is Forever: Learning to Live Again After the Loss of a Child*. New York: Valentine Books, 1991.

Brooks, A. M. *Grieving Time: A Year's Account of Recovery from Loss*. New York: Dial, 1985.

Caine, L. *Widow*. New York: William Morrow and Company Inc., 1974.

Cousins, N. *Anatomy of an Illness*. New York: Bantam Books, 1979.

Davis, D. *Empty Cradle, Broken Heart*. Golden, CO: Fulcrum, 1991.

Finkbeiner, A. K. *After the Death of a Child*. New York: Free Press, 1996.

Ginsburg, G. D. *Widow to Widow*. Cambridge, MA: De Capo Press, 1997.

Grollman, E. *Living When a Loved One Has Died*. Boston: Beacon, 1977.

Hewett, J. *After Suicide*. Louisville, KY: Westminster Press, 1980.

Hickman, M. W. *Healing After Loss*. New York: HarperCollins, 1994.

James, J. W., and F. Cherry. *The Grief Recovery Handbook*. New York: Harper Perennial, 1988.

Knapp, J. *Beyond Endurance: When a Child Dies*. New York: Schocken Books, 1986.

Kübler-Ross, E. *On Children and Death*. New York: Collier, 1983.

———. *On Death and Dying*. New York: Macmillan Company, 1969.

Kübler-Ross, E., and D. Kessler. *On Grief and Grieving*. New York: Scribner, 2005.

Kushner, H. S. *When Bad Things Happen to Good People*. New York: Schocken Books, 1981.

Limbo, R., and S. Wheeler. *When a Baby Dies*. Holmen, WI: Harsand Press, 1986.

Livingston, G. *Only Spring: On Mourning the Death of My Son*. San Francisco: Harper, 1986.

Lord, J. H. *No Time for Goodbyes: Coping with Sorrow, Anger, and Injustice After a Tragic Death*. Ventura, CA: Pathfinder, 1987.

Pausch, R., and J. Zaslow. *The Last Lecture*. New York: Hyperion, 2008.

Rando, T. A. *How to Go On Living When Someone You Love Dies*. New York: Bantam Books, 1991.

Rothman, J. C. *The Bereaved Parents' Survival Guide*. New York: Continuum, 2000.

———. *Saying Goodbye to Daniel*. New York: Continuum, 1995.

Schiff, H. S. *The Bereaved Parent*. New York: Penguin Books, 1977.

———. *Living Through Mourning*. New York: Penguin Books, 1986.

Schwiebert, P., and C. DeKlyen. *Tear Soup: A Recipe for Healing After Loss.* Portland, OR: Grief Watch, 2007.

Siegel, B. S. *Peace, Love and Healing.* New York: Perennial Library, 1990.

Swain, J. *On the Death of My Son.* Northhamptonshire, England: Aquarian Press, 1989.

BOOKS ABOUT OR FOR GRIEVING CHILDREN AND ADOLESCENTS

Adlerman, L. *Why Did Daddy Die?: Helping a Child Cope with the Loss of a Parent.* New York: Penguin Books, 1989.

Berstein, J. E. *Loss and How to Cope with It.* New York: Seabury, 1977.

Coburn, J. *Anne and the Sand Dobbies.* New York: Seabury, 1967.

Fassler, J. *My Grandpa Died Today.* New York: Human Sciences Press, 1971.

Fitzgerald, H. *Grieving Child: A Parent's Guide.* Hamden, CT: Fireside, 1992.

Gaffney, D. *The Seasons of Grief: Helping Children Grow Through Loss.* New York: Penguin Books, 1988.

Grollman, E. S. *Explaining Death to Children.* Boston: Beacon Press, 1967.

———. *Straight Talk About Death for Teenagers: How to Cope with Losing Someone You Love.* Boston: Beacon Press, 1993.

———. *Talking About Death: A Dialogue between Parent and Child.* Boston: Beacon Press, 1988.

Grootman, M. E. *When a Friend Dies: A Book for Teens About Grieving and Healing.* Minneapolis: Free Spirit, 1994.

Heegard, M. *When Someone Very Special Dies: Children Can Learn to Cope with Grief.* Minneapolis, MN: Woodland Press, 1988.

Krementz, J. *How It Feels When a Parent Dies.* New York: Knopf, 1982.

LaTour, K. *For Those Who Live: Helping Children Cope with the Loss of a Brother or Sister.* Omaha, NE: Centering Corporation, 1991.

LeShan, E. *Learning to Say Good-bye When a Parent Dies.* New York: Macmillan, 1976.

———. *When a Parent Is Very Sick.* Boston: Joy Street Books, 1986.

Rothman, J. C. *A Birthday Present for Daniel: A Child's Story of Loss.* Amherst, NY: Prometheus Books, 1996.

Schaefer, D., and C. Lyons. *How Do We Tell the Children?* New York: Newmarket Press, 1994.

Thomas, P. *I Miss You: A First Look at Death.* New York: Barrow, 2001.

Viorst, J. *The Tenth Good Thing About Barney.* New York: Atheneum, 1971.

Winsch, J. L. *After the Funeral.* New York: Paulist Press, 1995.

Helpful Websites

Again, this listing of websites is inevitably incomplete. However, those listed provide a good place to start if you are looking for information on such topics as serious illness, grief, and loss. Many of these organizations offer free educational materials; others sponsor local chapters with affiliated support groups. Several of the sites are also places that you might consider using to find a local therapist, support group, or hospice. Some of these sites also provide an opportunity to get involved in advocacy and/or fund-raising efforts.

American Academy of Child & Adolescent Psychiatry
www.aacap.org
> *This professional organization for psychiatrists has useful information on childhood or adolescent bereavement.*

American Association for Marriage and Family Therapy
www.aamft.org

This organization may serve as a potential resource to help find a family/marital therapist in your area.

American Association of Retired Persons
www.aarp.org

This organization has a grief and loss page with good information for bereaved adults.

American Association of Suicidology
www.suicidology.org

This organization provides multiple links to information related to suicide and maintains a directory of local support groups for survivors of suicide.

American Cancer Society
www.cancer.org

This organization, with many local chapters, provides information for cancer patients, their family members, cancer survivors, and care-takers.

American Family Therapy Academy
www.afta.org

This national family therapy organization may serve as another resource to help you locate a family therapist in your area.

American Hospice Foundation
www.americanhospice.org

This website provides useful information on both hospice care and grief.

A Place to Remember
www.aplacetoremember.com

This group provides support materials and resources for those affected by a complicated pregnancy or infant death.

Bereaved Parents of the USA
www.bereavedparentsusa.org

This is a national organization devoted to helping parents and families who have lost a child.

BreastCancer.Org
www.breastcancer.org

> *This nonprofit organization maintains an educational website on such topics as symptoms, diagnosis, treatment, and day-to-day coping with breast cancer.*

Centering Corporation
www.centering.org

> *This nonprofit organization maintains a listing of resources and readings on such topics as adult and childhood bereavement, along with infant loss and death of a child.*

The Compassionate Friends (TCF)
www.compassionatefriends.org

> *This self-help organization aims to support family members who have lost a child. They also have an extensive network of local support groups, educational programs, and materials.*

The Dougy Center
www.dougy.org

> *This website represents a national center for grieving children and families.*

GriefNet
www.griefnet.org

> *This website provides an Internet community of e-mail support groups for those dealing with serious illness, death, and/or major loss.*

Growth House
www.growthhouse.org

> *This website provides excellent resource information on most major grief-related topics.*

The Leukemia & Lymphoma Society
www.leukemia-lymphoma.org

> *This volunteer international organization is dedicated to funding research, education, and patient-support services. It maintains a patient call center and provides free educational materials on related subjects.*

Mothers Against Drunk Driving (MADD)
www.madd.org

This well-known organization provides educational materials and advocacy in their ongoing effort to prevent childhood death due to drunk driving incidents.

National Hospice and Palliative Care Organization
www.nationalhospicefoundation.org

This organization provides extensive information on such topics as hospice care, palliative care, advanced directives, caregiving, grief, and financial planning.

National Organization of Parents of Murdered Children, Inc. (POMC)
www.pomc.com

This national group provides emotional support, education, and advocacy for parents and families of a murdered child.

National Sudden Infant Death Syndrome Alliance (also called First Candle)
www.sidscenter.org

This national organization provides information on local support groups in addition to educational materials on infant safety and dealing with infant death whether through SIDS, miscarriage, stillbirth, etc.

Parents Without Partners
www.parentswithoutpartners.org

This international organization, with many local chapters, aims to provide companionship and idea exchange for those adults raising children alone, whether due to divorce, separation, widowhood, or never having been married.

Resolve
www.resolve.org

This national group aims to provide a community of support for women and men coping with infertility.

SHARE

www.nationalshare.org

> *This organization empowers the creation of local support groups and provides educational materials for parents who have lost a baby due to miscarriage, stillbirth, or newborn death.*

Soaring Spirits Loss Foundation

www.sslf.org

> *This national support network is for those grieving the loss of a loved one, with a special emphasis on widows and widowers. Its twofold purpose is to encourage peer support opportunities (both online and in person) and to provide resource information.*

RESOURCES FOR FAMILY CAREGIVERS

Alzheimer's Association

www.alz.org

> *This volunteer health organization is a world leader in Alzheimer's research and support. Local chapters offer a broad range of programs and services for those with Alzheimer's dementia and their caregivers.*

CaringBridge

www.caringbridge.org

> *This nonprofit organization offers free personalized websites that make it easier to share health updates and to receive supportive messages from family and friends while coping with a loved one's critical illness.*

Family Caregiver Alliance

www.caregiver.org

> *This agency provides educational support and advocacy information for family caregivers. Their services include help with care planning, legal/financial consultations, and respite care.*

Home Instead Senior Care

www.homeinstead.com

> *This is reportedly the world's largest provider of comprehensive, non-medical companionship and home-care services for aging adults. Of-*

fice franchises are located throughout the United States, Canada, Japan, Ireland, Portugal, and Australia.

National Alliance for Caregiving

www.caregiving.org

This organization represents a coalition of national organizations dedicated to providing support and information to family caregivers and to raising public awareness about family caregiving issues.

National Family Caregivers Association

www.nfcacares.org

This organization is dedicated to providing educational resource information and support for the millions of Americans who are caring for a chronically ill, aged, or disabled loved one. In partnership with the National Alliance for Caregiving, they have created a comprehensive online resource for family caregivers. It can be accessed at www.familycaregiving101.org.

Well Spouse Association

www.wellspouse.org

This is a national, not-for-profit membership organization created to address the needs of those wives, husbands, or partners who are caring for the disabled or chronically ill. Services include a complimentary monthly newsletter and assistance finding a local support group.

Young Cancer Spouses Organization

www.youngcancerspouses.org

The goal of this group is to bring together young spouses of cancer patients to share information, support, and experiences.

OTHER SUGGESTIONS

As you can see from the website listings, many chronic or life-threatening illnesses have their own national advocacy organization. An example would be the **American Cancer Society.** Most of these groups will have local chapters in major metropolitan areas, and they can be useful sources of either free educational pamphlets or available support groups, etc.

There are also national associations for many specific types of loss, such as **Resolve, The National Infertility Association,** or **Mothers Against Drunk Driving,** along with **Parents of Murdered Children (POMC)** and **First Candle** or the **National Sudden Infant Death (SIDS) Foundation.** Checking with your local library or community center, or online, will usually lead to many other opportunities for either local support or educational input.

HOW TO FIND A GOOD THERAPIST

If you decide to get additional help in the form of psychotherapy or counseling, there are several ways to approach finding the "right" therapist for you and/or your family. The best place to start is often via personal recommendation. This recommendation can come from one of your health-care providers, a friend who has experienced a similar situation, or your local minister or rabbi. A local oncologist or family physician has referred many of my private clients to me; others have come due to the recommendation of a prior client.

Additionally, most metropolitan areas will have nearby academic centers and teaching hospitals. Any of these institutions may have departments of psychiatry, psychology, social work, and/or behavioral medicine with listings of available private therapists. Many cities and larger towns will have local bereavement centers offering support groups and individual counseling, along with educational programs and materials. Most of these local grief centers also maintain listings of available and appropriately trained therapists in the nearby vicinity. Other possible avenues include consulting with your local chapter of an organization such as the **American Cancer Society,** the **American Psychiatric Association,** the **American Psychological Association,** or the **National Association of Social Workers.**

You will also want to check with your health-insurance provider to see what services or portion of services are reimbursable.

They may also have a listing of therapists in your local area that are approved by their network. Ultimately, you are looking for a therapist with appropriate credentials, training, and experience. But you are also looking for someone you feel comfortable with. So once you've made a list of several possible therapists, feel free to call and find out more about their practices. Think about what qualities are important to you. Do you care what gender or religion your therapist is? Is it important that a therapist has experience in working on illness or bereavement issues? Is this person available to see children, only adults, only individuals or families? Is he or she available at times that would be convenient for you, for example, evenings or weekends? Once you've identified someone you think might be workable, don't second-guess yourself: Just take a deep breath and make the first appointment. A good therapist will help you to get from there to where you need to go.

Although illness, death, and loss are all normal and inevitable parts of life, they are still usually challenging and even heartbreaking experiences. No one needs to go through these life crises totally alone. We all need and deserve help sometimes.

ACKNOWLEDGMENTS

Many heartfelt thanks to my agent, Gary Morris, and the folks at David Black Literary Agency for their willingness to take on a new author. I am similarly grateful to Hyperion editor Leslie Wells for her patient support as I learned along the way. This project would not have come about without the ongoing support and advocacy provided by both Jeff Zaslow (co-author of *The Last Lecture*) and Jai Pausch.

I also thank, from the bottom of my heart, all of the heroes represented in this book for the spirit of hope, courage, and wisdom that they allowed me to witness and now share with others. Last but certainly not least, my thanks to the colleagues, co-workers, good friends, and family members who were my steadfast cheerleaders during this amazing journey. I couldn't have done this without all of you.

91397